WHI
ARE OKAY
TOO

HEROES THROUGHOUT HISTORY

TIM CONSTANTINE

Voice of Reason
Publishing

Published by Voice of Reason Publishing, Washington DC
For information contact: Voice of Reason Publishing at
202-787-1911.

Illustrations and Caricatures by Marzio Mariani and
Oddonkey. Learn more at www.Oddonkey.com

Special thanks to Marzio Mariani, who created the delightful caricatures for this publication. His heartwarming portrayal of so many of history's important players added just the right touch of authenticity combined with a hint of levity to create the perfect balance for the book.

Marzio can be reached at oddonkey.com or through the publisher.

TABLE OF CONTENTS

INTRODUCTION

In the United States, the year 2020 had more racial and political strife than any year since 1968. The shocking and unnecessary deaths of Ahmaud Arbery and George Floyd stunned a nation. People of all races watched the video footage of the deaths and were appalled. The senseless killings galvanized a movement by an array of dissatisfied groups throughout the country. The seeds of discontent that had been sown and cultivated during the Obama years exploded in the summer of 2020.

Black Lives Matter, an organization that only four years earlier had openly led chants of "Kill the Police" and "What do we want? Dead Cops! When do we want it? Now!" suddenly became the mainstream voice for many dissatisfied citizens of all backgrounds and ethnicities. According to a Yahoo News-YouGov poll, support for Black Lives Matter among American adults grew from 27% in 2016 to 57% in 2020.

Anger and frustration boiled over. City blocks were burned to the ground. Police precincts were surrendered to the control of angry mobs. Statues were toppled. The racist label was retroactively applied to everyone from George Washington and Abraham Lincoln to Jesus himself. Tens of millions of dollars of damage and destruction to public and private property ravaged city streets from coast to coast.

In the midst of the mayhem, themes popularized during the Obama presidency came back to the forefront. Over a five year period politicians, athletes, movie stars and regular folks on social media all shared their anger and frustration with the perceived ills in society. Activists fanned the flames of division by race, by gender, by age and by ethnicity more than ever before.

The Oxford Dictionary defines the word "racism" as follows: Prejudice, discrimination, or antagonism directed against a person or people on the basis of their membership in a particular racial or ethnic group.

While it is clearly unacceptable to be a racist or misogynist, some believe there is an exemption for insults aimed toward one specific group, the white male. Over the past five years "old white men" have been called out, put down and threatened with an increasing regularity.

Salon, December 2015
White men must be stopped: The very future of mankind depends on it

TIME magazine, Feb. 2016
"The Old White Man's Last Hurrah"
If 2004 was the year of one angry white man screaming (Howard Dean), 2016 is the year of millions of angry white men and white voters in general screaming into the abyss

Paul Waldman, Washington Post, March of 2016
Hillary Clinton doesn't need white men.

December 2016 Bill Clinton
Trump knows how to get 'angry, white men to vote for him'

Huff Post, July 2017
OLD WHITE MEN SYNDROME
"I'd like to discuss a problem I feel we here in the USA seem to have that most other democracies do not. Old White Men Syndrome."

Don Lemon, CNN anchorman
"We have to stop demonizing people and realize the biggest terror threat in this country is white men"

Teen Vogue, teenage girls magazine
"Not only is white male terrorism as dangerous as Islamic extremism, but our collective safety rests in rooting out the source of their radicalization."

Economist Paul Krugman, New York Times
"The Angry White Male Caucus," in which he explains, "Trumpism is all about the fear of losing traditional privilege."

Actress Gabourey Sidibe, "The View,"
"Older white men are a problem, y'all, for everyone. We're all at risk."

Scary Mommy blog, Elizabeth Broadbent
Dear Entitled Old Racist White Men, We Are Sick Of You: This is no longer a country for entitled, asshole old men who think the world owes them something by virtue of their age and skin color. Sit down, old entitled white men. It's our turn now.

LeBron James - USA Today Dec. 2018
"In the NFL, they got a bunch of old white men owning teams and they got that slave mentality," James said. "And it's like, 'This is my team. You do what the (expletive) I tell y'all to do. Or we get rid of y'all.' "

Comedian Chelsea Handler via tweet
"Just a friendly reminder for the weekend: No white after Labor Day, and no old, white racist men after the midterms. Get out and vote."

The Root, February 2018
To All Old White Men Considering a Run for President in 2020: Reconsider

Washington Times, November 2019
Snoozefest 2020: Democrats bored with old white men as Hillary Clinton looms

Barack Obama, December 2019
Obama accused old white men running for office of "not getting out of the way." At a high profile event in Singapore Obama announced that women were

"indisputably" better leaders than men. If the whole world was run by women, Obama speculated, "you would see a significant improvement across the board on...living standards and outcomes."

Filmmaker Michael Moore, June 2020
"White men, a lot of white men, two-thirds of white men voted for Trump, feel that their grip on power is quickly fading -- it's being taken from them. They've been watching what's going on the past couple of weeks. They're just as angry at that cop in Minneapolis because he's really, he's really messed it up for the white male holding onto that power,"

The truth is there are good people and bad people of every race, gender and ethnicity. Equally true is that virtually all good men and women have said or done something they shouldn't have. None of us is without sin. Hopefully we are all judged by the body of our lifetime's work, not simply for any one act.

I have had the good fortune to travel to multiple countries in a wide variety of places around the globe including Asia, Africa and the Middle East. My experience has been that most humans are loving, giving people. Most respect their fellow man. Some however, primarily those who have been hurt or wronged, wish to strike out against others they perceive to be different or inferior.

I believe we are all God's children and thus must treat each other with respect. In *White Guys Are Okay Too* I have laid out key people throughout history in a wide range of categories. Most chapters start with a woman or minority who has excelled in that specific category. That is followed by a gentle, good-natured, fact based reminder to those who would bash old white men that white guys are okay too. Not better. Not superior, but not a threat to society either. There are things enjoyed and appreciated by millions around the world that are a reality because of some white guy somewhere. Penicillin, Coca Cola, the sport of basketball and air travel are just a few examples.

My Irish roots mean I am hard-wired to use humor to diffuse tension. My hope is that with this good natured look at heroes throughout history we can come together and better understand it is tough to have racism if we realize there is only one race. The human race.

- Tim Constantine

ON THE COVER

The cover of the book features people at the top of their professions from several different categories. Among those who appear on the cover are three Nobel Prize winners. One of those Nobel Prize winners is a woman. One is a black man. One is a white guy. All three are recognized among the greatest human beings of the 20th century. They were selected for the cover in a not so subtle reminder that greatness comes from all races, genders and ethnicities.

Mother Teresa

Mother Teresa, now recognized by the Catholic Church as Saint Teresa of Calcutta, founded the **Order of the** **Missionaries of Charity,** a Roman Catholic congregation of women dedicated to helping the poor. They established a hospice, a nursing home, centers for the blind, aged and disabled and a leper colony. Their work defined selflessness.

Mother Teresa was born as Agnes Bojaxhiu in Macedonia and grew up in a family dedicated to helping the less fortunate. Her mother regularly fed the poor and homeless at their family's dining table. As a child Agnes would ask her mother who the people eating with them were. Her mother's reply, "Some of them are our relations, but all of them are our people."

In 1979, Mother Teresa received the Nobel Peace Prize for her humanitarian work

Dr. Martin Luther King, Jr.

As a child Dr. Martin Luther King, Jr. attended segregated schools. He excelled in his studies early on and graduated high school at the tender age of fifteen. He went on to earn a Bachelor of Arts from Moorehouse College. In hopes of following in the footsteps of his father and grandfather, both of whom served as pastor of the Ebenezer Baptist Church in Atlanta, King attended the Crozer Theological Seminary. In what may have been a sign of things to come, Martin was elected president of his predominantly white senior class at Crozer and graduated as the 1951 valedictorian. He earned his Ph.D. from Boston University.

Dr. King became a board member of the National Association for the Advancement of Colored People (NAACP) in the mid 1950s and in 1955 took a leading role in the bus boycotts which led to a United States Supreme Court decision ensuring all people could travel on public buses as equals.

In the years that followed Dr. King traveled more than six million miles and gave more than 2500 speeches about injustice and inequality. He was arrested nearly two dozen times and was assaulted on at least four occasions. He was named Time magazine's Man of the Year in 1963. At the age of thirty five Martin Luther King, Jr. became the youngest person ever to be awarded the Nobel Peace Prize.

King was shot and killed outside his motel room in April of 1968 as he prepared to lead a protest march. He is generally recognized as the leader of the American civil rights movement and is a towering figure in 20th century history.

Albert Einstein

The name Einstein has become interchangeable with the term genius as a result of a lifetime of work by one Albert Einstein. He was originally trained as a teacher in physics and math but after graduating he had difficulty find a teaching gig. Instead he went to work at the Swiss Patent Office and continued his studies. In 1905 he earned his doctorate. It was Einstein's research and theories that led to a variety of earth changing creations including photoelectric cells, lasers, nuclear power, and fiber optics.

Einstein's best known research includes *Special Theory of Relativity* which he published in 1905, *General Theory of Relativity* which appeared in 1916, *Investigations on Theory of Brownian Movement* published in 1926, and *The Evolution of Physics* from 1938.

About the time Adolph Hitler was coming to power in Germany, Einstein emigrated to America to become the Professor of Theoretical Physics at Princeton, a post he held until his retirement in 1945. He became a United States citizen in 1940 and was offered the Presidency of the newly formed state of Israel in 1952. He declined.

The 1921 Nobel Prize in Physics was awarded to Albert Einstein "for his services to Theoretical Physics, and especially for his discovery of the law of the photoelectric effect."

Time magazine named Albert Einstein its "Person of the Century."

Three giants of the 20th century each impacted their fellow man in very different ways. Mother Teresa gave comfort to the poor and downtrodden. Martin Luther King, Jr. led peaceful change that assured a better life for generations to come. Albert Einstein was okay too.

White men, you know, are not all bad. Here's a short list: the white Founding Fathers; the white men who fought and died in the war that ended slavery; the white men who fought and died in WWI, WWII, Vietnam, Korea, Afghanistan, Iraq; and the all-white male Supreme Court justices who unanimously decided Brown v. Board of Education.

Larry Elder
National Talk Radio Host
The Boston Herald, 2018

CHAPTER ONE

– – –

MUSIC

Aretha Franklin

If you are ever at a family gathering and the room grows quiet in an awkward silence, there is one debate sure to get a lively conversation going. Who is the greatest vocalist of all time? The answer is simple of course, Aretha Franklin. Your crazy uncle can argue for Neil Diamond all he wants, but the fact is the range, the power and the command of Aretha Franklin's voice will never be matched. That might explain why she charted 77 singles in the Billboard Hot 100, including 17 top-ten singles. She sold more than 75 million records worldwide and won 18 Grammy Awards. She will always have the music industry's eternal R-E-S-P-E-C-T.

Aretha may have been the greatest among greats but the music industry has left ample evidence that some other guys were okay too.

Wolfgang Amadeus Mozart

Greatness in music is often judged by longevity of popularity. Do people still listen to an artist's music ten years later? Twenty? Is his or her music still heard fifty years after it was created? Did he influence other musicians? By those measures, one composer stands out among all others. Like so many successful artists, Mozart began to chase his passion for music at an early age. He enjoyed recognition and fame but seldom saw financial reward from it. Also like many legendary musicians, he died far too early under questionable circumstances. Two hundred and thirty years later his compositions are still enjoyed by millions. A superstar adored by fans that died too young? Mozart was a rock star before they even existed.

Elvis Presley

Arguably one of the most significant people of the 20th century, Elvis Presley was a superstar singer, movie actor and cultural icon. Possibly the first giant star to be recognizable by only one name, Elvis was the best selling solo artist of all time, with somewhere between 600 million and 1 billion in music sales. He holds the record for the most songs on Billboard's top 40 with 115. According to the Rock n Roll Hall of Fame, Presley spent 80 weeks at number one on the charts, more than any other artist. He holds the RIAA record for the most gold albums with 101 and the most platinum albums with 57. Incredibly two more recently released Presley albums both reached number one in the United Kingdom in 2015 and 2016, nearly 40 years after his death. Elvis Presley will forever be The King.

Frank Sinatra

If one were to open Webster's Dictionary to the word "charisma" Frank Sinatra's picture would appear. Ol' blue eyes, as he became known, enjoyed massive success in music and at the cinema box office. His voice and his icy blue eyes certainly contributed, but it was his undeniable level of cool that cemented his place as the legend he remains to this day.   Sinatra sold over 150 million records worldwide. He won an Academy Award for *From Here to Eternity* (1953) and was widely respected as a film actor. He could walk into any room and be the center of attention, even among Presidents. He actively campaigned for Presidents Truman, Kennedy and Reagan. Always bigger than life, at one point Sinatra was investigated by the FBI for his alleged ties to the Mafia. After Frank's death in 1998 at age 82, music critic Robert Christgau referred to him as "the greatest singer of the 20th century."

Elton John

Combine outlandish onstage antics with a tremendous voice and a knack for composing music to any lyric presented to him and you have one of rock's greatest showman, Elton John. Whether he was dressed as Donald Duck or Wolfgang Amadeus Mozart, an Elton John concert always promised to simultaneously be a spectacle and a musical delight. His unmatched achievements include seven consecutive number-one albums in the United States.

Sir Elton was knighted by Queen Elizabeth II in 1998. In addition to Grammy Awards, his music has earned him an Academy Award, a Tony Award and a Golden Globe. He has sold more than 300 million records. His rewritten version of *Candle in the Wind* was dedicated to Princess Diana and sold more than 33 million copies, the best selling single in the history of the music charts.

U2

If a rock 'n roll band starts out with an extremely limited level of success, what is the logical step for them to take to jump start their efforts? Most people would probably not answer "Dedicate their life to Christ" and yet that is exactly what U2 did. Three of the four band members decided early in their careers that God was an important part of who they were and that their work would reflect it. Management was less than enthusiastic, but it seems to have worked out okay. Forty years later U2 has sold more than 150 million records worldwide and their only peer in concert ticket sales is The Rolling Stones. They were inducted into the Rock n Roll Hall of Fame in their first year of eligibility, still espousing their beliefs, with Bono explaining to the Rock Hall crowd of industry insiders that the song the band was about to play *Until the End of the World* was about Jesus and Judas. The crowd laughed. Bono paused and repeated with stone cold seriousness, "This song is about Jesus and Judas". For now at least, U2 continues to deliver rock 'n roll heaven right here on earth.

The Rolling Stones

Rock 'n roll fans tend to fall into one of two distinct categories: The Beatles or The Stones. Some will tell you the Beatles are the greatest band ever, and the band's ten year run was certainly legendary. The Rolling Stones however, have a very different story. 58 years after forming in London, The Stones enjoyed yet another number one song in 2020 with the timely *"Living in a Ghost Town"*.

Defying all odds, most doctors and probably a guardian angel or two, Keith Richards continues to thrive in his late seventies along with bandmates Mick Jagger, Charlie Watts and Ronnie Wood. Possibly the only band that can sell out football stadiums on a moment's notice regardless of price, The Rolling Stones continue to build on a legacy that includes three of the highest grossing tours of all time, 30 studio albums, 23 live albums and 120 singles. If aliens landed on earth and demanded a three minute explanation defining rock 'n roll, one would need only play the Stones' classic song *(I Can't Get No) Satisfaction* and the question would be answered.

CHAPTER TWO

LITERATURE

To Be, Or Not Toobe?

Cai Lun

Who you think the best author of all time is depends completely on your personal taste. Do you prefer fiction or non-fiction? Do you like an uplifting read or a stomach churning thriller? There is one person that is the undisputed champion however when it comes to influence on literature. Cai Lun was born in China, just one generation after Jesus wandered the earth. Lun endured an extended rough patch early in life, serving as a court eunuch for nearly 15 years. Eventually he was promoted and was placed in charge of manufacturing instruments and weapons. At the age of 55 Cai invented the composition for paper and perfected the paper-making process. For his successful and world-changing efforts the Emperor gave Cai an aristocratic title and lots of money.

The original paper-making process included the use of materials like bark, hemp, silk, and fishing net. Cai Lun's exact formula has been lost, possibly because someone focused a little too much on the hemp. When unexpected palace intrigue resulted in a change of emperor, Cai chose to take his own life. There is no official word as to whether he used his own invention to leave behind a suicide note.

Though it was an ancient Chinese inventor who made it all possible, a review of literature history will find that among those who utilized Lun's invention, there is an extensive catalog of other guys that have proven to be okay too.

William Shakespeare

To be or not to be, that is the question. Shakespeare chose to pursue a career in writing and ultimately became widely known as the finest English language writer in history. It was almost not to be as Shakespeare was involved in the 16th century's version of a shotgun wedding when he was just 18 years old. Six months later he and his much older bride welcomed twins into the world. Being a family man did not squelch his creativity however. Best known as a poet and a playwright, Shakespeare was successfully paying the bills and feeding his family from his craft before the age of thirty. His early works were primarily comedies and histories. While they are well regarded, it was his later work writing such tragedies as *Hamlet, Othello* and *Macbeth* that assured his place in literature history.

Though he died at the relatively young age of 52, William Shakespeare's works include 39 plays and 154 sonnets. His plays have been translated into every major language currently spoken on planet earth.

Charles Dickens
Most people would certainly recognize the titles *A Christmas Carol, Oliver Twist, Great Expectations* and *A Tale of Two Cities*. Ebenezer Scrooge, Tiny Tim and David Copperfield are all characters that are as familiar to many people as their own family. Most however, may not realize these characters were created and their stories were written between the years of 1837 and 1861.

Born and raised in England, Dickens enjoyed something highly unusual for his era, frequent international travel. He enjoyed extensive trips through the United States, Italy, France and Switzerland. His success and fame also allowed him to pioneer reading tours. His first such tour included 129 appearances in 49 different towns throughout England, Scotland and Ireland. While he was known for the words he crafted rather than playing music, Dickens was in some ways the original rock star.

Ernest Hemingway

Ernest Hemingway was a tortured soul who lived anything but an ordinary life. He was wounded while serving in World War I. He married four times. In the 1930s he made Key West his home and later took up residence in Cuba. He was an unabashed Castro supporter. Hemingway also developed a reputation as a heavy drinker. While in Africa in 1954 Hemingway was involved in two plane crashes in two days. Near the end of his life he suffered from depression and paranoia and ultimately killed himself.

Why then has Ernest Hemingway made it onto the list of impressive purveyors of literature? He published seven novels, six short-story collections, and two nonfiction works. Hemingway won a Pulitzer Prize for Fiction for his 1952 book *The Old Man and the Sea*. He won the Nobel Prize in Literature in 1954. Three of his novels, four short-story collections, and three nonfiction works were published after his death. Many consider his works to be classics of American literature.

Stephen King

Sometimes referred to as "The King of Horror" Stephen King has published nearly sixty novels, six non-fiction books and somewhere in the neighborhood of two hundred short stories. He is hard-wired to write and practices his craft daily. Where as some people may choose to jog three miles a day, King writes at least 2000 words as part of his daily routine. Some of what he writes blossoms into wildly popular stories. Some never sees the light of day. The

formula seems to work pretty well. King has sold more than 350 million books in thirty three languages. Much of the world knows King through movie adaptations of his writing. Among the most successful King films are *The Shining, Shawshank Redemption* and *Stand by Me*.

Just prior to the launch of his 2017 film *IT* a single red balloon floated in the window of King's Bangor, Maine mansion. The spooky stunt got plenty of attention and the movie grossed over $700 million at the box office.

His mother apparently taught him to share his toys because King's Foundation gives away over $2.8 million annually to a variety of causes including schools, libraries, fire departments and to pay the winter heating bills for Maine families in need.

CHAPTER THREE

MOVIES

Spike Lee

There are a handful of film directors that have shaped both Hollywood and the movie going public's perception. Spike Lee's production company, 40 Acres and a Mule Filmworks, has produced more than thirty five films since 1983. Lee's films *Do the Right Thing, Malcolm X, 4 Little Girls* and *She's Gotta Have It* were each selected by the Library of Congress for preservation in the National Film Registry for being "culturally, historically, or aesthetically significant."

Nearly all of the work Lee has written and directed explores race relations, black culture, urban life including crime and poverty and the role of media in the world today. He has garnered a variety of awards for his work including an Academy Award, two Emmy Awards, two Peabody Awards and the Cannes Grand Prix. Ironically Spike Lee is best known by some people for the Nike commercials he wrote, produced and starred in with Michael Jordan, "It's gotta be the shoes."

While no one can dispute Spike Lee's influence on film and pop culture, here are a few other guys that have had an okay impact on Hollywood too.

Sean Connery

One of the most successful franchises in the history of film is James Bond. Twenty seven Bond movies have grossed more than $7 billion in sales. The most popular Bond actor by most accounts is Sean Connery. He starred in seven films in the franchise and set the standard with his witty one liners, crazy stunts and exotic locations that all Bond actors followed thereafter. He enjoyed success in several other Hollywood productions as well, including *The Hunt for Red October* and *The Rock*. He won an Academy Award for *The Untouchables*.

In 1989, at the age of 59 he was proclaimed "Sexiest Man Alive" by People magazine, and in 1999, just a few months short of his 70th birthday, he was voted "Sexiest Man of the Century".

John Wayne

Few actors have personified the American values of their era the way John Wayne did. Typically cast as a cowboy or soldier, always patriotic and in the industry parlance of the time, a "good guy", Wayne enjoyed Hollywood success for more than forty years. He earned an Academy Award for Best Actor in 1970 for his work in *True Grit*.

Even after his death at age 79 John Wayne remained a powerful figure in American culture. He was awarded the Congressional Gold Medal, the Presidential Medal of Freedom and the Naval Heritage Award posthumously. In 1999 the American Film Institute included John Wayne on their list of the Greatest Male Screen Legends. In an age where the word "icon" is tossed around casually, one need only look to John Wayne to fully understand its intended definition.

Sylvester Stallone

Best known for his self created roll of the fictional boxer Rocky Balboa, Sylvester Stallone has brought joy to tens of millions of people around the globe as an actor, director and producer in the film industry. Long before he was a household name, Stallone wrote the script for *Rocky* and attempted to sell it to multiple Hollywood studios. He was offered $350,000 for the rights to the film, but the studio intended to use Robert Redford or Burt Reynolds in the lead role. Stallone refused to sell unless he could play Rocky Balboa himself. The studio eventually agreed and *Rocky* went on to be nominated for ten Academy Awards. It won three including Best Picture.

The concept of the movie franchise proved to be Stallone's path to riches and success. Not only did the *Rocky* franchise turn out seven successful films, Stallone made five *Rambo* films and three *Expendables* movies. Because the characters he portrayed were often muscle bound, strong, quiet types, some assumed Stallone was no genius himself, but he wrote or co-wrote most of the films in the three franchises and directed many of them.

Steven Spielberg

Perhaps someone somewhere would argue that Steven Spielberg isn't the most successful director in the history of Hollywood. The person making that argument would be wrong. The list of films and film franchises that Spielberg has directed is unparalleled. *Raiders of the Lost Ark, Jaws, Jurassic Park, Saving Private Ryan* and *E.T.* are just the tip of the iceberg. His ability to translate a story to film in such a way that audiences are entertained is proven not only by box office ticket sales, but how well nearly all of his work stands the test of time.

Spielberg's success is testament to the power of perseverance. He was a poor student in high school and as a result was turned down admission to the University of Southern California (USC) not once, not twice but three times. Like a Hollywood movie with a happy ending however, the director became a member of the Board of Trustees for USC in the late 1990s. His one major career disappointment? He has been turned down twice to direct James Bond movies.

Robert Redford

Robert Redford has enjoyed success as both an actor and director. His boyish good looks put him in Webster's Dictionary in the 1970s as the very definition of handsome. *The Sting, The Great Gatsby* and *All the President's Men* were some of his most popular films. Redford made the Sundance Film Festival a reality. It is the largest independent film festival in the U.S.

Redford's career spanned more than sixty years and he won multiple awards including two Academy Awards (one for

Lifetime Achievement). He was awarded the National Medal of Arts, he received Kennedy Center Honors and was honored with a Presidential Medal of Freedom in 2016. Perhaps even a larger statement than any honor he has received is that fact that The University of Southern California School of Dramatic Arts now has an annual award named for him, The Robert Redford Award for Engaged Artists.

Tom Cruise

Worldwide box office ticket sales approaching $9 Billion make Tom Cruise an A-list celebrity of the top tier. For more than thirty years Cruise has been as close as Hollywood gets to guaranteed success. The number one movie in the year 1986 was Cruise's *Top Gun* with $179 million in sales. That was big money for the era. His most recent film in the *Mission: Impossible* franchise grossed $791 million at the box office. His good looks, his characters' cocky attitude and his ability to laugh at himself in real life have all contributed to his staying power.

If you were to remove Tom Cruises' work from the history of film, the disappearance of movies such as *Risky Business, Top Gun* and *A Few Good Men* would leave a tremendous void. His active role in The Church of Scientology seems to bother some people, but their attention might better be spent acknowledging his work as an international advocate, activist and philanthropist in the fields of health, education and human rights.

CHAPTER FOUR

– – –

CULINARY ARTS

Chocolate

The desirability of any given culinary dish is completely subjective. What one person enjoys, another may find repulsive. There are a few items that seem to appeal to nearly all of humankind the world over. At the top of that list may well be chocolate. The origins of chocolate can be traced to the ancient Olmecs of southern Mexico, who in turn passed it on to the Aztecs. It was originally a bitter beverage with very little in common with our modern day sweet treat.

In the 21st Century it is not uncommon for people to binge on chocolate. Folklore tells us the most notorious chocolate lover of all was the mighty Aztec ruler Montezuma II who allegedly drank gallons of chocolate each day for energy and as an aphrodisiac, possibly inspiring the much later invention of Pepto Bismol.

In 1847 the first chocolate bar was created in Britain and was made from sugar, chocolate liquor and cocoa butter. Swiss chocolatier Daniel Peter added dried milk powder to chocolate in 1876 and several years later worked with Henri Nestle to bring milk chocolate to the masses. Today you have dozens of chocolate bar choices every time you check out at the grocery or convenience store.

Food Canning

Paris Chef Nicolas Appert began experimenting in the late 1700's on how to preserve food and extend it's useful life. By 1810 he was selling his idea to Napoleon and the French government. Appert would place food inside glass jars, cork them kind of like wine and then seal off the container with a wax seal. He would wrap the food jars and then finally boil them. Two years later an Englishman, Brian Donkin, came up with an even better idea. Glass jars were breakable. Tin was not. Presto! The tin can became the vehicle for Appert's process. The world of food preservation was forever changed.

In an odd quirk, the can opener wasn't invented until 1858, which makes one wonder if there were cans of food sitting unopened for 40 years. According to food expert Jerry James Stone it wouldn't have mattered even if there were. Apparently canned food has always been remarkably safe. In 1974, according to Stone, food samples were taken from cans found on a steamboat which sank nearly 100 years prior and the food was found completely safe to eat. Desirable? Not so much. But it was safe.

McDonald's
It is not often that one hears the phrase "culinary arts" and the name McDonald's in the same breath, but in our context of major impact on the world, McDonald's restaurants have had as big of an impact as anyone. The official McDonald's history goes something like this:

In 1917, 15-year-old Ray Kroc lied about his age to join the Red Cross as an ambulance driver, but the war ended before he completed his training. He then worked as a piano player, a paper cup salesman and a Multi-mixer salesman. In 1954 he found a small but successful restaurant run by brothers Dick and Mac McDonald. The brothers produced a limited menu, concentrating on just a few items – burgers, fries and beverages – which allowed them to focus on quality and quick service. Kroc saw an opportunity. In 1955, he founded McDonald's System, Inc., a predecessor of the

McDonald's Corporation, and six years later bought the exclusive rights to the McDonald's name and operating system. By 1958, McDonald's had sold its 100 millionth hamburger. Today McDonald's has more than 37,000 outlets in over 100 countries worldwide. They serve more than 69 million customers every day.

Potato Chips

George Crum, who was half African and half native American, was working as a cook at a resort in Saratoga Springs, New York in 1853 when he created the first potato chips, or so the story goes. Years later his sister claimed that she had invented the tasty snack. History tends to believe it was George who did the creating.

Either way it wasn't until the 1920's that chips gained any popularity. An American businessman from North Carolina named Herman Lay began selling potato chips to grocers across the south out of the trunk of his car. By 1938, Lay was so successful that his Lay's brand chips went into mass production. Ultimately Lays Potato Chips became the first successfully marketed national brand.

The next giant step in potato chip marketing came in the 1950's when the owner of an Irish chip company named Joe "Spud" Murphy figured out how to create flavored seasoning and add it in during the cooking process. Two early flavors were Cheese & Onion and Salt & Vinegar. According to Healthy Beginnings magazine, potatoes have become America's number one snack food in one very specific form, a thin, salted, crisp chip.

Breakfast Cereal

Cold cereal is America's favorite breakfast food, with approximately 1 in 3 people choosing it as their go-to meal to start the day. How cereal came to such popularity is a great study in fate. In 1863 Dr. James Caleb Jackson invited a number of people to a vegetarian wellness retreat. He encouraged his guests to try his concentrated grain cakes. They weren't particularly tasty, but the healthy aspect appealed to one of his guests, who happened to be prominent in the Seventh Day Adventist Church. She made his "Granula" part of the church doctrine. As fate would have it, one of the early members of the church was a gentleman by the name of John Kellogg.

John Harvey Kellogg was a doctor and trail blazer in the concept of health food. He was in charge of the Battle Creek Sanitarium in Battle Creek, MI. Using Jackson's Granula as his starting point, Kellogg created a biscuit of oats, wheat, and corn. You probably know it by the common name granola.

Kellogg and his brother, Will Keith Kellogg, experimented with many breakfast ideas including boiling wheat and rolling it into sheets, then grinding it. One night they completely forgot about a pot they had boiled. When they returned in the morning they discovered their error and tried to roll it out anyway. The wheat berries came out as hundreds of flakes. Undaunted, the Kelloggs toasted the flakes and more than 125 years later people are still enjoying the fruits of their forgotten pot of wheat.

Donuts

Perhaps the most decadent of all culinary treats is the dough fried ring. Typically donuts are flavored or decorated in some tempting way that appeals to the sweet tooth in all of us. Among the most popular toppings are sugar, chocolate or maple glazing. Dutch settlers brought large balls of sweetened dough with them to New York in the early 1800s. These dough balls did not yet have the distinctive ring shape but laid the groundwork for later success.

It was in 1847 that a sixteen year old boy, working in the kitchen of a lime-trading ship, began punching holes in the center of dough in an effort get rid of the greasiness of the popular snack cake. Hanson Gregory's effort resulted in the ring we are all familiar with today. He shared his creation with his mother, who in turn, made them a popular success. Gregory himself went on to enjoy a career as a sea captain. Dunkin' Donuts and Krispy Kreme will be eternally grateful to the young man from Camden, Maine.

Kool Aid

Take a packet of flavored powder, mix it with sugar and water, toss in some ice and presto! You have one of the great summer beverages for kids everywhere. Today Kool-Aid is owned by Kraft Heinz and sells millions and millions of dollars worth of the tasty powdered treat every year but the origins of the brand are considerably more humble.

Edwin Perkins created Kool-Aid in 1927 in his mother's kitchen in Hastings, Nebraska. At the time there was a popular liquid concentrate called Fruit Smack. The trouble with the flavored liquid was shipping costs. Perkins discovered a way to remove the liquid and reduce Fruit Smack down to a powder. He called this powder Kool-Aid. Perkins started producing his powder in high quantity and by 1931 had outgrown Nebraska, moving his entire operation to Chicago. General Foods bought him out in 1953. In retirement Perkins found himself spending his days relaxing and drinking, what else? Kool-Aid. Oh yeah!

CHAPTER FIVE

STATESMEN

Nelson Mandela

The word statesman is defined in the dictionary as someone who is a leader in national or international affairs, a person whose wisdom and integrity win great respect. Perhaps no one better exemplifies the combination of all these factors than Nelson Mandela.

Mandela worked as an attorney in Johannesburg as a young man. In the 1940s he became active in the African National Congress (ANC) and fought against the then new policy of apartheid. He was repeatedly arrested in the 1950s and by 1961 found himself sentenced to life in prison for conspiring to overthrow the state. He handled his arrest and conviction with amazing grace and dignity. During the 27 years he was in jail, he was offered freedom from the prison, with certain conditions, on six different occasions by the apartheid government. He declined each time.

In 1990 South African President F.W. de Klerk, under tremendous pressure and the threat of civil war, released Nelson Mandela from prison. Together the two led efforts to negotiate an end to apartheid. In 1994 Mandela led the ANC to election victory and became South African President himself. The primary focus of his term in office was reconciliation of his country's racial groups. Mandela declined a second term as President. As an elder statesman he led the fight against HIV/AIDS in South Africa.

Nelson Mandela was seen by some on the right as a trouble maker and terrorist. His efforts at bringing people together were frequently criticized by those on the left for being too eager to negotiate and forgive. Through it all Mandela maintained a dignity and wisdom seldom seen on the international stage. He received more than 250 honors and awards for his work including the Nobel Peace Prize.

George Washington

George Washington was a military general, a Founding Father and the first President of the United States. Prior to leading the new nation, Washington had been nominated by Benjamin Franklin to preside over the Constitutional Convention that resulted in the US Constitution, a document that though amended, is still followed today.

The late rock star Tom Petty once sang "The Waiting is the Hardest Part" and George Washington could be exhibit A to prove the point. Under the Constitution, state electors voted for the first President on February 4, 1789. Congress was required by law to convene within one month to tally the votes. March 4 came and went without Congress being able to gather a quorum. Finally on April 5 a Congressional quorum was reached and the count found that Washington had won the majority of votes in every state. He was inaugurated on April 30, 1789 complete with a marching band, a thirteen gun salute and more than 10,000 people looking on. It was pretty impressive for a country that had only recently come into existence.

George Washington opposed political parties, preferring instead a unified effort for the common good. In a forerunner of what is now known as the America First policy, Washington emphasized the United States must concentrate on its own interests. His assertion that "religion and morality are indispensable supports" seems to fly in the face of 20th century Supreme Court rulings calling for stark separations between church and state.

One of the great leadership qualities of George Washington was his willingness to do anything he asked his men to do. As General, he commanded thousands of troops, yet relished the heat of battle himself. According to early American historian John Clement Fitzpatrick, Washington had two horses shot out from under him in one well-known military campaign and both his hat and his coat managed to suffer bullet holes. The man himself however, went unscathed.

Abraham Lincoln
Abraham Lincoln led America through its greatest political crisis in history, the Civil War. He managed to preserve the Union, abolish slavery and strengthen the federal government in the process. It's easy to recite facts about the civil war era without fulling appreciating the depth of the crisis. The country was literally disintegrating. Southern states were quitting. The union of states was no longer united. To the political observer of the day it would have been a logical conclusion that the country would never survive to celebrate a 100th anniversary.

Lincoln managed to balance the wants and needs of both Republicans and Democrats, while appealing directly to the public for nationalism, equal rights and democracy. He was intimately involved in strategy planning during the civil war. He also ran his own reelection campaign. He was the architect of the end of slavery with his Emancipation Proclamation. Lincoln ordered that the Army protect

escaped slaves and was a strong proponent of the Thirteenth Amendment. He followed his conscience.

Abraham Lincoln's tragic assassination forever ensconced him in American folklore, but it was his brilliant actions in the face of the most dire circumstances that assured his place in history as one of America's greatest Presidents.

Winston Churchill

Winston Churchill is best known for teaming with Franklin Delano Roosevelt and Joseph Stalin to defeat Adolph Hitler and the Nazis in World War II. While that was certainly the apex of his career, Churchill lived a robust roller coaster life full of ups and downs. Born into wealth, but lacking in attention from his parents, Churchill was a poor student. He went into the military and by the age of 26 had written five books. In 1900 he joined the House of Commons as a Conservative. The causes he championed were anything but conservative. He wanted an eight hour work day, a minimum wage and public health insurance. By 1904 he had become a Liberal. As a young man he was known to be provoking at times and developed a reputation for poor judgement during World War I and the years that followed.

Churchill was outspoken in his criticism of the Nazis after they came to power in 1933. He advocated for an aggressive stance against them, but initially his warnings were largely ignored. In 1938 Prime Minister Neville Chamberlain acquiesced to some of Hitler's requests in an effort to appease Germany and stay out of their way. Once Hitler invaded Poland, Britain and France were forced to declare war. Neville Chamberlain was pushed out of office and Winston Churchill became Prime Minister in May of 1940. Along with his US and Russian counterparts he shaped Allied strategy in World War II. Despite the Allies ultimate victory, Churchill and his Conservative party were tossed out of office by the voters just two months after Germany's surrender in 1945.

Churchill won the Nobel Prize for Literature in 1953 in the midst of his second go around as Prime Minister. Some modern historians compare U.S. President Donald Trump to Churchill because both were perceived as egotistical and self-absorbed. Big ego or not, Churchill left an indelible mark. In 2002 the BBC polled nearly half a million Brits and Sir Winston Churchill was selected as the Greatest Briton of All Time.

Ronald Reagan
Ronald Reagan was the 40th President of the United States and by many polls, the most popular President since at least World War II. His early career in radio and Hollywood movies translated well in his political life. His extraordinary public speaking ability earned him the nickname, The Great Communicator.

Reagan was elected as President of the Screen Actors Guild in 1947, a post he would be reelected to six times. He played a key role in getting residuals for television actors when their episodes aired again as re-runs or in syndication. After a stint with General Electric that required him to appear on television and as a motivational speaker, Reagan began to get serious about politics. He was elected Governor of California in 1966 and reelected in 1970.

Reagan beat the sitting President of the United States, Jimmy Carter, in 1980. At the time of his election he was branded by opponents as a cowboy and war-monger. Ironically he would prove to be exactly the opposite, negotiating the first ever reduction in nuclear weapons with the Soviet Union. He is also generally credited with bringing about the fall of the Berlin Wall. Reagan's reelection as President in 1984 earned him the most electoral votes of any U.S. President ever with 525. His 97.6% of the Electoral College was a remarkable landslide.

Reagan inherited a disastrous economy from the Carter administration with record high inflation, interest rates and very high unemployment. "Reaganomics" not only turned the economy around, it resulted in the largest peace time economic expansion in U.S. history at that point in time. When Reagan left office in 1989 his approval rating stood at 68%. Only Franklin Delano Roosevelt had ever had a departing approval that high. The one big difference was that FDR left in a hearse. Reagan rode off into the sunset on horseback.

Pope John Paul II

Pope John Paul II was elected as Pope at the age of 58. He was chosen at the second papal conclave of 1978, a result of the unexpectedly short thirty three day reign of his predecessor Pope John Paul. The second Pope chosen that year was from Poland, the first non-Italian Pope in 455 years. He immediately captured the imagination of people all over the globe with his relative youth and vigor. Pope John Paul II enjoyed skiing and football among other activities. An assassination attempt on the Pope in May of 1981, during which John Paul was shot four times, took a toll on his athletic endeavors. It failed to slow down the Pope's worldwide peace mission however. He visited 129 nations in an effort to promote greater understanding and cooperation between various countries and religions.

His visits drew tremendous crowds whether traveling to Africa, North America or any other corner of the globe. On one visit to Mexico he drew an audience estimated at five million people. Pope John Paul II continued to draw people to him and to God until the very end. More than three million people paid their final respects at St. Peter's Basilica after his death in April of 2005. Pope John Paul II was declared a Saint by the Holy Catholic Church in 2014.

CHAPTER SIX

\- \- \-

THE OLYMPICS

Jesse Owens

Jesse Owens was the first Olympic track and field athlete to win four gold medals in a single Olympics. His remarkable performance in the 1936 Olympic Games would not be equalled until Carl Lewis did it in 1984. What made Owens' effort most memorable however was that it happened not only during a time of deep segregation in his own United States, but at an Olympics hosted by Adolph Hitler in Nazi Germany. The amazing performance shattered Hitler's master race theory and proved that individual excellence can come from any person, regardless of race or national origin.

Owens' tremendous talent became apparent early. While competing in track and field at his Cleveland high school Owens equaled the world record in the 100 yard dash and he long-jumped 24 feet 9 inches. He went to college at Ohio State. At the Big Ten Conference Championships in 1935, Owens broke three world records and tied a fourth, all in just 45 minutes. It still stands as the greatest hour in sporting history,

The greatest track and field athlete of all time took up the then-trendy habit of smoking cigarettes at the age of 32 and quickly became a pack-a-day man. In late 1979 he was hospitalized with a very aggressive form of lung cancer. By the end of March 1980 Jesse Owens died at just 66 years old. Jesse was awarded the Presidential Medal of Freedom, the highest award bestowed upon a civilian, by President Gerald R. Ford, symbolizing America's recognition of his important role in history. His tremendous speed and athleticism were outpaced only by his grace and dignity.

Fate cast Jesse Owens as an Ambassador to the world and he embraced the role perfectly.

Ray Ewry
Ray Ewry isn't exactly a household name, but if Olympic greatness is measured by the number of gold medals an athlete earns, Ewry has to be on the list of the best ever. He competed in three different Olympic Games from 1900 to 1908 and earned eight gold medals. He also earned two gold medals in the 1906 Intercalated Games in Athens, Greece. Ewry had contracted polio as a young boy and required the use of a wheelchair, making him not only one the greatest Olympic athletes of all time, but one of the most unlikely as well.

Ewry used various squatting and jumping exercises as therapy to overcome his polio. He strengthened his legs so well that when he went to Purdue University he joined the football team and ran track and field. His graduate degree in engineering took him to New York and there he became a member of the New York Athletic Club. In his Olympic efforts Ewry won the gold medal in every event in which he ever competed.
To put Ray Ewry's level of achievement in perspective consider the following. His eight Olympic gold medals in individual events remained the most by any athlete for more than 100 years. The remarkable record was finally broken by swimming phenom Michael Phelps in 2008.

Emil Zatopek

Emil Zatopek was a long distance runner immortalized by his performance for the Czechoslovakian Olympic team in 1952. Zatopek won the gold medal in the 5000 meter and 10,000 meter races. He then made a last-minute decision to enter the marathon, an event he had never run before in his life. He not only won the gold medal, he set an Olympic record for the event in the process.

Zatopek happened upon his running prowess quite by accident. At the age of 16 he was randomly pulled off the line at the shoe factory he was working at and told to compete in a race. He initially objected, claiming he was too weak. A Doctor said otherwise and after that initial race Zatopek never looked back. Just four years later he was setting a variety of Czech long distance running records. By 1949 he had broken the 10,000 meter world record twice, and went on to better his own record three times over the next four seasons. He also set records in the 5,000 meters, 20,000 meters, the one hour run, 25,000 meters, and 30,000 meters.

Emil earned a reputation as an extremely friendly guy during his time in international competition and his ability to speak six languages helped him develop lifelong friendships with many other athletes. In February 2013, *Runners World* magazine selected Zatopek as the Greatest Runner of All Time.

Michael Phelps

The most decorated Olympic athlete of all time is American swimmer Michael Phelps. Over the course of competing in five Olympic Games Phelps won 28 medals, including a record 23 gold. At the 2008 Games in Beijing he became the first athlete to win eight gold medals at a single Olympics, breaking Mark Spitz's 1972 record of seven.

During his competitive heyday Phelps practiced world class levels of both eating and training. He claimed in a 2008 interview to eat 12,000 calories a day, including up to two pounds of pasta and full pizzas. The food was fuel for his legendary workouts, purported to have lasted five hours per day, six days a week. The routine seems to have worked. During his career Phelps set 39 world records, which is a record all by itself.

When he retired from competitive swimming in 2016 Michael Phelps had won more Olympic medals than 161 countries. Today Phelps enjoys time with his wife and three sons and volunteers full time as a swim coach at Arizona State. Most sporting experts consider him the greatest swimmer ever.

CHAPTER SEVEN

TECHNOLOGY

The Magnetic Compass

The Chinese lay claim to what they refer to as the Four Great Inventions from ancient China. Among them is the magnetic compass. It was first invented as a device for divination as early as 206 BC and was improved and adopted for navigation by the Chinese of the 11th century. The magnetic compass works by pointing its needle to magnetic north, allowing the user to navigate direction in a simple and accurate manner.

In the 21st century devices like smartphones all come equipped with GPS technology that uses satellites to direct a person not only through the wilderness, but through metropolitan city streets. When the great electro magnetic pulse comes and renders all powered technology useless however, or if you simply don't have access to power for your phone or GPS unit, the compass will still show humans the way.

The magnetic compass remains a great symbol of ancient China's advanced science and technology. A few caucasian men have had some technological breakthroughs along the way that turned out okay too.

Thomas Alva Edison

Thomas Alva Edison has been described as America's greatest inventor. Among his inventions were the phonograph, the motion picture camera and the first practical electric light bulb. He held 1,093 US patents in his name. He established multiple research laboratories including one in Fort Myers, Florida in collaboration with Henry Ford and Harvey Firestone. Edison would keep teams working in shifts, 24 hours a day. He slept at random hours and wanted a full staff available to work with him at any hour, day or night. He pioneered the concept of scientific teamwork.

Thomas Edison developed hearing problems at an early age. The cause of his deafness has been blamed on a variety of reasons. Some say a childhood illness, likely scarlet fever, damaged his inner ears. Edison himself changed his explanation for his condition several times. He once claimed a train engineer struck him on the ears, rendering him mostly deaf. Regardless of the origins, being completely deaf in one ear and barely hearing in the other didn't slow Edison down.

Thomas Edison began work in 1878 on a system of electrical illumination, His intention was to create something to compete with gas and oil-based lighting that was safer and easier to use indoors. After more than a year of experimentation, Edison found carbon filaments to be the best material to achieve his goal. His first real success came in late 1879 when he developed one light that lasted 13.5 hours. He filed for a patent in November of that year, and continued to tinker with the design. In 1880 Edison realized a carbonized bamboo filament could last over 1,200 hours.
Edison made the first public demonstration of his incandescent light bulb on December 31, 1879, inadvertently setting into motion the tradition of lighting up the night at midnight every New Year's Eve.

Galileo
Over the last fifty years there have been no shortage of celebrities recognized by a single name including Cher, Madonna and Bono. None have had a bigger impact than

one of the original one name wonders, Galileo. Among other things, Galileo made the telescope practical and usable and he invented an early type of thermometer. He was a philosopher, astronomer and mathematician.

In 1609 Galileo Galilei began observing the heavens with instruments that magnified up to 20 times. His telescopes showed the moon's surface was rough and uneven and not made of cheese. Galileo discovered the four biggest moons of Jupiter, the rings of Saturn and put forth the idea that the earth orbits the sun. That last one was considered heresy by the Roman Catholic Church who at the time was quite sure that earth was literally the center of the universe.

For the trouble of all his great discoveries Galileo was sentenced to life in prison. He was allowed to serve out his time under house arrest. He died at home at the age of 77.

James Watt

The railroad is often cited as the key to the economic engine that powered the economy of early America and the world. The real question is what powered the railroad? James Watt created the steam engine in 1769, leading to dependable power for engines and pumps for factories, steamships and locomotive trains. The trains ran on the railroad, which could be expanded nearly anywhere.

Watt's invention allowed trains to carry people, products, livestock and building products to previously unreachable destinations. The steam engine is widely credited as beginning what would become the industrial revolution. Steam tractors helped farmers plow bigger areas more efficiently. Factories used steam power to get machinery to do the work of dozens of men. James Watt's invention made life easier and opened up opportunity that previous generations hadn't even dreamed of.

Alexander Graham Bell

Alexander Graham Bell's mother and his wife were both deaf, fueling his passionate research on hearing and speech. His father, his grandfather and his brother all worked on elocution and speech, so in many ways the telephone sprouted out of the family business. Bell worked extensively as a private tutor. Among his students was Helen Keller. It was his experimentation on hearing devices that eventually led to Bell getting the first U.S. patent for the telephone in 1876.

Bell had not been the only person working on voice transmission at the time and there were some who claimed he had stolen their research and technology. Over a period of 18 years, the Bell Telephone Company faced 587 court challenges to its patents, including five that went to the U.S. Supreme Court. None was successful. In fact the Bell Telephone Company never lost a case that proceeded to trial.

According to GSMA Intelligence there are 5.24 billion people that have a mobile telephone device on earth today. AT&T is among the top five business brands recognized worldwide. AT&T generates $181 billion per year.

The Wright Brothers

The Wright Brothers, Orville and Wilbur are best known for having invented the world's first successful motorized airplane. On December 17, 1903, near Kitty Hawk, North Carolina the brothers had their first successful flight lasting a total of 12 seconds. The following two years they improved their invention to make longer flights with increasing control. It was their third design, the Wright Flyer III that was the first that could be termed as practical.

In their early years the Wright brothers had learned and practiced their mechanical knowledge working in a shop with bicycles, printing presses and motorized machinery. Their work with bicycles in particular, impacted their belief that balance and control was the key to successful air flight. They spent about three years flying gliders and learning how to control an aircraft. The knowledge they gained from that practice led to the creation of a three-axis control system, which essentially allowed a pilot to steer an aircraft. While the technology has changed dramatically, their method of control remains standard on airplanes to this very day.

In the modern era much of the science of aerodynamics and wind drag coefficients is established with the use of wind tunnels. Nearly 120 years ago the Wright Brothers used a homemade wind tunnel to develop consistent data for wings and propellors. Whether you're driving a sleek modern automobile or flying with your family for vacation, you have Orville and Wilbur Wright to thank.

Tim Berners-Lee

Contrary to his famed claim, former US Vice President Al Gore did not invent the internet. A gentleman by the name of Tim Berners-Lee actually came up with the platform that was the foundation for the world wide web all of us use on a daily basis. In 1989 Berners-Lee was seeking a more efficient way of communicating with his colleagues. He wanted research scientists to be able to share their results, techniques, and practices without the cumbersome requirement of each communique happening one email at a time. He created a way in which each could deposit information online and others could instantly access that information anytime they wished. He wrote the software for the first Web server.

Berners-Lee gradually expanded the uses of his creation, intentionally making it as simple to use as possible. He hoped it would be appealing and useful to the widest audience that way. By 1994 he established the World Wide Web (W3) Consortium at the Massachusetts Institute of Technology's Laboratory for Computer Science, which provides oversight to the Web and the development of standards.

If you were to draw up a fictional biography for the character that had created the world wide web, you would be hard pressed to come up with a more impressive resume than Tim Berners-Lee. He received a first-class degree in physics from Oxford University. He was then contracted by CERN, the European Organization for Nuclear Research. CERN's purpose is fundamental physics, finding out what the Universe is made of and how it works. It is no small irony that Berners-Lee had such a colossal impact on how our human universe works.

In March of 2011, Tim Berners-Lee was one of the first three recipients of the Mikhail Gorbachev Award for "The Man Who Changed the World" at the inaugural awards ceremony held in London.

CHAPTER EIGHT

— — —

BUSINESS & INDUSTRY

Oprah Winfrey

Oprah Winfrey first gained fame for *The Oprah Winfrey Show*, the highest-rated television program of its kind in history. It ran in national syndication for 25 years. With unmatched business acumen, Winfrey has parlayed her television success into a multi-billion dollar business empire. She was declared the richest African American of the 20th century. Her personal net worth is estimated to exceed $3 billion, making her the richest self-made woman in America. Life for Winfrey however, could not have started out more differently.

Born to a poor teenage single mother in rural Mississippi, Winfrey had a rocky start. After struggling during her early teens in inner city Milwaukee she moved to join her father in Nashville and dramatically turned her life around. She became an honors student, was voted most popular girl, and joined her high school speech team. At age seventeen Winfrey won the Miss Black Tennessee beauty pageant and the local black radio station, WVOL hired her to do the news part-time. She worked there during her senior year of high school and in her first two years of college. In 1983 she went to Chicago to host a half-hour morning show called *AM Chicago*. She was an immediate hit. Movie critic Roger Ebert encouraged Winfrey to sign a syndication deal with King World and in 1986 *The Oprah Winfrey Show* began to broadcast nationwide.

Oprah leveraged her fame and maximized her brand in a variety of ways. She co-founded the cable television network Oxygen. She became President of her own production company. In 2006 she signed a three year $55 million dollar deal with XM Satellite Radio to establish a new radio channel. In 2008 she formed her own network, Oprah Winfrey Network. In 2015, Winfrey purchased a minority stake in the publicly traded company Weight Watchers for a reported $34 million. By 2020 the value of those shares had increased to as much as $430 million. Oprah.com averages more than seventy million page views per month.

Her influence and success cannot be overstated. She was awarded the Presidential Medal of Freedom by President Obama and has received an honorary doctorate degree from Harvard. Oprah Winfrey is generally regarded as the most successful business woman in the history of the world.

Henry Ford

Certain events in history forever change the way humankind lives and works. Henry Ford, born during the Abraham Lincoln administration, was instrumental in one of those major changes. He is generally recognized for having created the manufacturing production line using standardized, interchangeable parts. A look at Ford's automobile production shows what a huge impact his innovation had. In 1908 Ford introduced the Model T. The factory output was 100 cars a day. As he perfected the moving assembly line the numbers grew dramatically and by the time Ford stopped production of the Model T nineteen years later, they had produced 15.5 million of the cars in the United States, almost 1 million more in Canada, and another 250,000 in Great Britain. Ford also developed the idea of a franchise system. The result was Ford dealerships throughout most of the United States and eventually on six continents.

Early in his professional career Henry Ford became the chief engineer at the Detroit Edison Company main plant. It was the responsibility of Ford and his team to make sure electricity stayed on 24 hours a day. They were literally always on call. Ford used this irregular schedule to his advantage and spent much of his time experimenting. His goal? He wanted to build a gasoline powered engine. By the end of his first year at Detroit Edison he had succeeded. Ford sold that first engine in order to finance his efforts at improving his creation. He sold the second so he could work on a third. So it went for nearly ten years before Henry Ford had an automobile he felt was ready to sell to the public. He used a primitive form of what we now call crowd funding to raise $28,000. The rest, as they say, is history.

Coca Cola

Coca Cola was invented in the late 19th century by John Pemberton. Pemberton was an injured Civil War veteran who became addicted to morphine. Realizing this was a problem, Pemberton set out to find an alternative. He created a beverage that included coca leaves and kola nuts. You can figure out the name from there. Essentially he created a drink with cocaine and caffeine as its two primary ingredients. He marketed the drink as a great elixir, claiming it would cure not only morphine addiction but indigestion, headaches and impotence. The first Coca Cola sales were made in Atlanta in 1886. Pemberton died suddenly in 1888 and his son Charley took over the business.

Sadly Charley Pemberton was an alcoholic and opium addict. Recognizing opportunity, businessman Asa Griggs Candler bought out Pemberton. Records indicate Candler paid less than $2000 for the brand. He used new and aggressive marketing techniques to position the brand to dominate the world soft-drink marketplace. Coca Cola continued this practice throughout the 20th century. On September 12, 1919, Coca-Cola Co. was purchased by a group of investors for $25 million.

Coca Cola has continued its marketing campaign to this very day. The soft-drink was the first commercial sponsor of the Olympic games (1928) and during the last fifty years Coca-Cola has sponsored the FIFA World Cup, Major League Baseball, the NFL, the NBA, and the NHL. In 2015 Coca Cola was named the third most valuable brand on the planet, behind only Apple and Google. It is estimated that consumers drink nearly two billion Coca Cola products around the world every day.

The cocaine was removed from the formula in 1903.

IBM
IBM has a dozen research laboratories on six continents worldwide. The company has scientists, engineers, consultants, and sales professionals in over 175 countries. It holds more patents than any other U.S. based technology company and employs more than 350,000 people around the globe. Year after year IBM is listed among the best places for employees, employees of color and women to work. The tech powerhouse can trace its roots back to the late 1800s. The first dial recorder was invented by Dr. Alexander Dey in 1888. The Bundy Manufacturing Company became the first time-recording company in 1889. The Computing-Tabulating-Recording Company (rolls right off the tongue doesn't it?) brought these companies and others together under one corporate umbrella in 1911. Thomas J.

Watson joined the company in 1914 and under his guidance it quickly became the industry leader. In the 1920s the company added electric typewriters and a variety of other office machines into its catalog and changed its name to International Business Machines (IBM).

IBM has played key roles in a wide range of world changing events including the first Moon landing in 1969. It provided computers and personnel to help NASA make history. Do you want your eyesight improved? In 1981 the LASIK surgical procedure was developed by two IBM scientists. Late on your Christmas shopping? Never fear. 46% of all Christmas season holiday consumer sales are now made online. How did that happen? In 1997 IBM literally created the term eBusiness and the framework to make it a reality.

IBM employees have earned five Nobel Prizes and five National Medals of Science.

Bill Gates - Microsoft

Bill Gates is best known as the co-founder of Microsoft Corporation. During his career there he held a variety of positions including Chairman, CEO, president and chief software architect. In the early days of Microsoft Gates created and licensed an operating system to IBM, the biggest computer company in the business at the time. With the MS-DOS operating system Gates became indispensable to IBM. In the mid-1990s he turned Microsoft's development efforts toward consumer and enterprise software.

Gates was seemingly always destined for greatness. He wrote his first software program at the age of thirteen. Later he and some friends computerized their high school's payroll system. The same group founded Traf-O-Data, a traffic-counting system, which they sold to local governments. Gates and friend Paul Allen, both quit Harvard University in order to start Microsoft. The choice seems to have worked out pretty well.

Bill Gates was awarded the Presidential Medal of Freedom in 2016.

Steve Jobs - Apple

The company we now know as Apple, Inc. was founded in 1977 by Steve Jobs and his high school pal, Steve Wozniak. Their first product was the Apple II, which was an instant success. By 1981 Apple had a huge initial public offering of stock and two years later became the fastest company to make it into the Fortune 500. Despite all the success, Jobs was pushed out of Apple in 1985 by a CEO he himself had recruited.

In 1986 Jobs became the majority stockholder in a computer graphics firm called Pixar. In the years that followed, Pixar became enormously successful with hit movie after hit movie, including *Toy Story, Monsters, Inc.* and *Cars*. It was actually Pixar, not Apple, that made Jobs a billionaire.

Apple's Board of Directors, finding their company in deep trouble, reached out to Steve Jobs in 1997 and asked him to come back and lead the company again. He forged a new direction for their computers but it was his vision on consumer electronics that set Apple on the path to colossal levels of success. It was under Jobs that Apple introduced iTunes and the iPod, revolutionizing the music industry in the process. In 2003 Apple started selling music downloads and by 2006 they had sold more than one billion songs and videos. 2007 saw Jobs introduce the iPhone, completely changing the playing field for cell phones.

Steve Jobs was diagnosed with cancer of the pancreas in 2003. He fought the deadly disease for years. In 2009 he had a liver transplant due to liver cancer. He continued to serve as CEO of Apple for two more years before health forced him to resign in August of 2011. Two months later he was dead at the age of fifty six.

Jeff Bezos - Amazon
Amazon.com was started by Jeff Bezos in 1994 with $10,000 from his own pocket. At the time the company was completely run out of his garage working on desks made out of doors purchased from Home Depot. During the first month of business, Bezos fulfilled and shipped orders to all 50 states and to 48 countries. Books were the only product. The key was the brand new world of the internet, which allowed Amazon to carry more books than the typical bricks and mortar store and to deliver nearly anywhere on the planet. One popular Bezos story is how the early computer servers used so much power in their home that Jeff and his wife couldn't run a hair dryer without blowing a fuse.

Bezos took the company public in 1997 at a valuation of approximately $300 million. The next year Amazon started selling music and videos. Customers could listen to short music clips before buying, which was unheard of in a physical music store. They also offered 125,000 music titles, far more than any mall store could possibly carry. Amazon spent an enormous amount of time, effort and money on keeping their customers happy. They also focused on growth. By 2020 Amazon's stock price had risen enough to give the company a valuation in excess of $1.5 trillion. It was only the second company ever to achieve value in the trillions.

Today Amazon has 647,500 employees, occupies 288.4 million square feet of real estate and accounts for nearly half of all online retail sales in the United States. Bezos is considered the wealthiest person in the world with a 2020 estimated worth of about $185 billion. Not bad for a guy who originally wanted to name his company Cadabra.

CHAPTER NINE

AGRICULTURE

The Cotton Gin - Eli Whitney

Late in the 18th century the average cotton picker could remove the seeds from about one pound of cotton per day. A man named Eli Whitney changed that with his cotton gin and in the process change agriculture forever.

Whitney's father before him had been a farmer so he had an appreciation for the work that went into planting, growing and harvesting a crop. After graduating from Yale College in 1792 Eli Whitney found himself accepting a job on a plantation near Savannah, Georgia. It was there he learned about cotton production and the difficulty cotton farmers had making a living. He patented his cotton gin in 1794. It greatly sped up the process of removing seeds from the cotton fiber. With his creation, a team of two or three workers could produce around fifty pounds of cotton in a single day. Sadly there was little honor among plantation owners of the day and rather than buy one of Whitney's inventions, many stole his design and constructed their own machines. The cotton gin changed agriculture forever but it made very little money for Eli Whitney.

It was not a wasted effort for him however. Based in part on his successful creation, Whitney later got a contract with the United States government to build muskets. Again he revolutionized the world of industry, this time by making standardized interchangeable parts, a new idea at the time. Not only did this make for faster assembly, it made it possible to repair the muskets rather than replace them.

Eli Whitney is universally recognized as a pioneer of American manufacturing.

The Steel Plow - John Deere

According to agricultural corporate giant John Deere, their founder was a typical blacksmith. He worked on hayforks, horseshoes and other common needs of the day. He learned hard work first from his Dad, then as an apprentice and eventually Deere opened his own blacksmith shop. In 1837 he took note that wooden and cast iron plows weren't working very well. Prairie soil had a sticky clay that tended to gum up the plow, slowing down work and sometimes damaging equipment. He remembered polishing needles at his father's tailor shop by running them through sand and wondered if a similar approach would work with plows. After some experimentation he found highly polished steel plows with a particular shaped moldboard could handle the soil much better.

John Deere sold three of his new plows in 1839. The old wooden plow had taken 24 hours to plow one acre. John Deere's steel plow took only five to eight hours. In 1843 he filled 400 steel plow orders and by 1849 he produced 2000 plows. In the ensuing years John Deere would develop multiple models of plows and continue to grown his business.

John Deere became a millionaire selling his steel plows, an extraordinary feat considering the era. Perhaps even more impressive however is the impact John Deere continues to have to this day. In 2019 John Deere generated about $39.26 billion in net sales and revenue.

Milking Machines

The United States produced over 217 billion pounds of milk for human consumption in 2019. That is a lot of cows and a lot of milking. How is it even possible? Milking machines.

Mankind has long milked cows for dairy products but it wasn't until 1860 that Lee Colvin invented the first hand-held pumping device. This was followed in 1879 by Anna Baldwin's large rubber cup that attached to a cow's udder and to a pump lever and a bucket. Her concept was sound but it wasn't practical. It hurt the cow. It did however lay the groundwork for future milking machines that would prove more efficient.

The first mechanized milking system for dairy cows actually came from New Zealand. Norman Daysh, a dairy farmer himself, made a product that eased the workload of farmers and was comfortable for the cow. So confident in his invention was Daysh that he offered farmers a 100% return guarantee if they were not happy with it. None were returned. Many of the basic principles of his creation remain in modern milking technology today.

CHAPTER TEN

— — —

SPACE

The International Space Station
There may be no better example of the human capacity to work together regardless of race, gender or country of origin than the International Space Station (ISS). It is a partnership of space agencies including those from the United States, Russia, Europe, Japan and Canada. The station is divided into two sections: the Russian Orbital Segment, operated by Russia and the United States Orbital Segment, which is shared by many nations. It has been continuously occupied since November 2, 2000. Over the years more than 230 individuals from 18 countries have visited the International Space Station, at least 34 women among them. Several black astronauts have flown to the ISS and worked on it. The ISS even hosted one visitor from the United Arab Emirates.

The International Space Station orbits earth about every hour and a half, which means astronauts see a sunrise 15 times a day. Does their time in space affect the astronauts? At least one ISS experiment suggests space has an effect on even the simplest of living things. In November 2008, 250 cherry tree stones were taken to the International Space Station. They orbited the Earth over 4,000 times before being returned to the planet in July 2009. They were planted in fourteen widely varied locations, By 2014 one sapling at the Ganjoji Temple in Japan had grown to thirteen feet tall and had produced several flowers, six years earlier than expected. The flowers had five distinct petals. Normal would be thirty. Similar results were recorded at three other locations.

While the International Space Station clearly demonstrates that all humans can and should contribute to our collective science and knowledge, it was a fairly small group of pioneers that laid the groundwork making human advancements in space possible. Those pioneers are okay too.

Robert H. Goddard
Born in 1882, Robert H. Goddard became fascinated with the idea of space travel after reading the H.G. Wells' science fiction novel *War of the Worlds* as a teenager. He was the first to prove that rockets can propel in an airless vacuum like space and was also the first to explore mathematically the energy and thrust potential of various fuels, including liquid oxygen and liquid hydrogen. It was Goddard who made the fictional dreams of space travel a potential reality when he successfully launched the world's first liquid-fueled rocket on March 16, 1926.

The Hubble Telescope

The telescope is named after astronomer Edwin Hubble but was actually conceived by Lyman Spitzer. He first proposed his concept of telescopes operating in outer space in 1946. Spitzer's contributions to science are legendary, but they may not be as strong as his gift for patience. Hubble wasn't launched until 44 years after he first suggested it. It was worth the wait. Spitzer analyzed photos from the space telescope for NASA until his 1997 death at the age of eighty three.

Hubble's orbit outside the distortion of Earth's atmosphere allows it to take extremely sharp images with almost no background light. Initially estimated to cost $400 million. Hubble's actual total completed cost was closer to $2.5 billion. Money well spent? The science says yes. Over six thousand scientific journals have been created based on info from Hubble.

Early Space Travel

On April 12, 1961 Soviet cosmonaut Yuri Gagarin became the first man in space when he went around the Earth once inside the Vostok 1 capsule. A little more than three weeks later the United States puts its first astronaut, Alan Shepard, into space. On February 20, 1962 John Glenn became the first American to orbit Earth, completing three revolutions aboard Friendship 7.

Moon Landing

Neil Armstrong descended down the ladder of the lunar orbital vehicle Columbia, uttered a few words about one small step and became the first man to walk on the moon. He was followed by Buzz Aldrin. Crew member Michael Collins had the heartbreak of being told "Wait here. We'll be right back." The date was July 20, 1969. People back on earth were riveted as the event unfolded. Global viewership was estimated at more than 550 million viewers, a world record at the time.

Many years later Buzz Aldrin would joke that when the crew was passing through US Customs after their journey, they had to declare they were carrying moon rocks and moon dust samples.

CHAPTER ELEVEN

— — —

HIGHER EDUCATION

University of Oxford
Times Higher Education World Rankings comprises the world's overall, subject and reputation rankings for the finest universities. They have said Oxford is the top university in the world. Forbes World University Rankings has also been known to place Oxford at the top of their list. Every reputable university ranking system puts Oxford in the top five. It is tough to beat such a track record. The collegiate research university has been around since the late 11th century in one form or another. That makes it the oldest university in the english speaking world.

Oxford's rich and lengthy history has helped establish it among the most prestigious learning institutions, which in turn has also made it one of the most influential. It has produced an extraordinary list of alumni including twenty eight United Kingdom prime ministers. It's not cheap to maintain such an impressive run. Oxford took in more than $3 billion in 2019 including $782 million in research grants and contracts.

Harvard University
The oldest institution of higher learning in the United States is Harvard University. It was established during the Puritan era in 1636. Its first benefactor was a gentleman named John Harvard and thus the name. When he died he left half his estate to the new school along with his extensive library. Many would argue it is the finest university in the United States.

Harvard is not without some cracks in its impressive history. In the early 20th century Harvard President A. Lawrence Lowell tried to limit the number of Jews that could attend

Harvard. During Lowell's tenure the University also established the Secret Court. It was made up of five Harvard administrators for the expressed purpose of rooting out homosexual activity. The Secret Court interviewed more than 30 students, faculty and alumni. Eight students were expelled from Harvard by the court. One alumnus had his association with the university revoked and one faculty member was dismissed.

Harvard counts seven United States Presidents among its alumni including John Adams, John Quincy Adams, Rutherford B. Hayes, Theodore Roosevelt, Franklin D. Roosevelt, John Kennedy and Barack Obama.

Yale University
There are always some people who think they can do better than the status quo. Such was the case with the Puritans in the Massachusetts Colony in the mid-1600s. Some split off and created their own community in what is now known as Hartford, Connecticut. In the decades thereafter some drifted south to New Haven. Several were alumni of Harvard and realized they needed to have their own institution of higher learning. In 1701 Yale College was born, making what is now known as Yale University the third oldest in the United States.

Yale's roots were Christian. Not only were ten clergymen instrumental in the organization and founding of the school, Christianity was at its very core for about two hundred and fifty years. In the last fifty years or more however, Yale has largely severed any formal ties to faith in Christ.

Like other universities that routinely appear at or near the top of the various lists of the best schools, Yale has graduated a number of impressive leaders including U.S. Presidents William Taft, Gerald Ford, George Bush, Bill Clinton and George W. Bush.

University of Phoenix

Oxford, Harvard and Yale may be considered among the best but the University of Phoenix is generally regarded as the largest private university. It was created specifically to provide higher educational opportunities for working adults.

The University of Phoenix started offering classes in 1976. It was founded by John Sperling with the same traditional classroom setting as most universities. Sperling wanted to allow adults to earn a degree while still working full time. Early rules included a minimum age of 23, some work experience and some college credit. The concept was largely successful and with the creation and growth of the internet, the University of Phoenix blossomed nationwide. Eventually online courses became the primary focus and the school changed its requirements to allow anyone with a high-school diploma or equivalent to attend.

The University of Phoenix went public with a stock offering in 1994 which brought in a huge amount of money and allowed rapid growth to occur. School records indicate there were more than 100,000 students enrolled in the year 2000. By 2010 that number had grown to somewhere in the neighborhood of 500,000 students. It made the University of Phoenix the largest for profit school in the United States. The university offered instruction within eight colleges and schools and allowed students to earn associate's, bachelor's, and master's degrees as well as doctorates.

The University of Phoenix generates big money. It is estimated that at one point as much as 85% of the school's revenue came from federal student loan programs. In 2015 that statistic caught the attention of the Federal Trade Commission. They opened an investigation. The result was a serious contraction of the student population. Though it currently has less than 200,000 students no one can argue with the fact that the University of Phoenix has opened the door to higher learning to millions of adults.

CHAPTER TWELVE

— — —

TELEVISION

Eddie Murphy

Eddie Murphy is the funniest person in the history of American television. All due respect to Seinfeld and Kelsey Grammar. Both provided laughs to audiences for years and years, but when a nineteen year old Eddie Murphy joined Saturday Night Live, he was fresh, different and quite frankly, saved the SNL franchise. Murphy did great impersonations, created memorable original characters and did quirky interpretations of classic television personalities like Mister Rogers and Buckwheat.

Murphy could be child-like and innocent or he could be raunchy and crude. Regardless, he made you laugh. He jumped from television to movies and largely ruled supreme in the world of comedy throughout the 1980s. Among his hits were *48 Hours, Trading Places* and *Beverly Hills Cop.* Along with his success and fame, Murphy managed some stumbles along the way. He fathered nine children with five different women. He had an embarrassing run-in with police in 1997. Through it all Murphy remained wildly popular with the American public. In late 2019 when Eddie returned to Saturday Night Live for the first time in 35 years, the show scored its largest audience in more than a decade. That episode demonstrated two things. Murphy was still the funniest man on television and America still loved him.

Milton Berle

Only 35,000 television sets were in use in the United States in 1948. By 1950 that number had exploded to six million and a decade later the industry estimates there were sixty million TVs in America. Needless to say with the soaring popularity of the new medium came opportunity. Few capitalized on the opportunity more than Milton Berle. He was the first major American television star and was known to millions of viewers as "Uncle Miltie" and "Mr. Television."

The beauty of Berle's time on NBC's Texaco Star Theatre was that because it was completely live it was often unpredictable. Berle sometimes comically appeared in women's clothing. He is widely credited for fueling the growth of television sales during the era. He was popular with his home audience and equally popular among some of Hollywood's leading ladies. Marilyn Monroe was among those he spent intimate time with.

Milton Berle was among the first inductees into the Television Academy Hall of Fame in 1984.

Ron Howard
Regardless of your age the chances are you've been entertained by Ron Howard. He first gained national attention in 1960 playing Opie Taylor on *The Andy Griffith Show*. The show aired through 1968. In 1974 Howard was cast as Richie Cunningham on ABC's *Happy Days,* where he remained a star until he chose to leave the show in 1980. With two hit series under his belt and still only in his twenties, Howard made a calculated decision to move his work behind the camera. He took to directing, producing and writing. Howard wrote and directed for both television and films. His biggest success came at the box office. Among his films are Cocoon (1985), Backdraft (1991), Apollo 13 (1995) and A Beautiful Mind (2001). He won the Academy Award for Best Director and the Academy Award for Best Picture with A Beautiful Mind.

Two giants in television history shared the camera during a 1982 Saturday Night Live episode. Ron Howard was the guest host. In the now classic comedy sketch, Eddie Murphy played the role of an interviewer who refused to acknowledge Howard's directing career, instead focusing on his childhood acting roles. Murphy eventually conflates the two most famous Howard characters and leads the audience in chants of "Opie Cunningham! Opie Cunningham!" Pure genius.

Ron Howard was inducted into the Television Hall of Fame in 2013.

Johnny Carson

21st century television is littered with late night talk show hosts, each clamoring for attention with his own unique brand of humor. Jimmy Fallon, Jimmy Kimmel, Conan O'Brien and all the others owe any success they enjoy to one man, Johnny Carson. The King of Late Night, as Carson was known, defined the late night genre and dominated the airwaves for three decades. To put that in perspective, if any of today's hosts get three million viewers it is considered a success. Johnny Carson's farewell episode drew more than fifty million.

Carson's attraction to entertaining people began when he was just twelve years old. He got a mail order magician's kit, practiced his new found craft and began to perform in public. By the age of fourteen he was making $3 per show, no small sum for a kid in 1939. By the early 1950s Carson was hosting a morning television show that lampooned local politics. It was on that show that Carson honed a unique skill, being funny without being mean spirited. This would become his hallmark throughout his career. Carson moved to New York City in 1957 to take hosting duties on ABC's *Who Do You Trust?* His likable personality, informal interview style and quick wit spelled success year after year. In 1962 NBC asked Carson to take over their late night program when Jack Parr retired. At first Carson declined but eventually agreed to take the gig and ultimately changed television forever. He became the highest paid person on TV and helped launch the careers of Jay Leno, Roseanne Barr, Ellen DeGeneres, David Letterman, Tim Allen and Jerry Seinfeld.

Even Carnac the Magnificent couldn't have foreseen the level of success Johnny Carson would achieve.

Alex Trebek
The Answer is: Fourteen. The correct question is: What is the number of people it takes to create and assemble the categories and clues for each episode of *Jeopardy*? The current version of the popular game show has aired more than 8000 episodes, won thirty three Daytime Emmy Awards and garnered a Peabody Award. A huge part of that success has come compliments of emcee Alex Trebek. Since the 1984 revival of the show Trebek has handled hosting duties for *Jeopardy!* Prior to that he captained

several game shows including *The Wizard of Odds, Battlestars, Classic Concentration* and *To Tell the Truth.* Trebek hosted one other popular game show for a single episode when he switched places with *Wheel of Fortune* host Pat Sajak as an April Fool's Day prank in 1997.

As a young man Alex Trebek hoped to pursue a career in broadcast news. While still working on his college degree the Canadian native took a job with the CBC. Little did he know he'd eventually earn his fame and fortune sharing factual information on a daily basis, but in a format that required the answer as the question.

In 2019 Morning Consult did a national poll and found *Jeopardy!* and Trebek ranked as the most popular game show and most popular host respectively. More than half said they couldn't imagine watching the show without him.

Homer Simpson

Homer Simpson is fat, bald, lazy, not very bright, frequently drunk and perpetually puts his own wants ahead of the needs of his family, yet he is one of the most popular people in all of television. He has one advantage few others in his line of work enjoy. He isn't real.

Homer Jay Simpson is the father character in The Simpsons, an animated sitcom now in its fourth decade of production for Fox. The show is set in the fictional town of Springfield and makes a good natured mockery of American culture. Homer first appeared on television in 1987. Cartoonist Matt Groening created the entire Simpson family. He said he chose Homer's name for the Dad because it was his own father's name.

The Simpsons phenomena is worldwide. The British newspaper *The Sunday Times* described Homer as "The greatest comic creation of our time". In 2010 Entertainment Weekly named Homer as the greatest character "of the last 20 years". The Simpsons has won twenty seven Emmy Awards and been nominated for sixty more.

William Shatner

Remaining active and productive as an actor for any period of time is difficult, yet for more than sixty years William Shatner has been coming into your home in a variety of roles. After being trained as a classical Shakespearean actor at the Canadian National Repertory Theatre, Shatner took several television gigs including guest spots on *Alfred Hitchcock Presents, The Twilight Zone* and *Route 66*. It was his starring role as Captain James T. Kirk of the USS Enterprise on *Star Trek* (1966-1969) that catapulted him to the stratosphere of fame.

His notoriety as Captain Kirk was so great it actually hampered Shatner from finding ongoing acting work for a number of years after *Star Trek*. Throughout the 1970s he took guest roles on established television programs to pay the bills. He appeared on *The Six Million Dollar Man, Columbo, Ironside* and *Mission: Impossible* among others. Shatner landed the title character role in ABC's *TJ Hooker* (1982-1986). As he aged he became a pitch man for various products and services including priceline.com. His character Denny Crane first appeared on ABC's *The Practice* before being spun off into it's own program *Boston Legal* (2004-2008). Crane was pompous, rude and undeniably funny. Many of the character's lines were ad libbed by Shatner in the moment during filming.

In 2020 at the age of 89, Shatner re-entered the dating market after divorcing his fourth wife. Court papers at the time showed he was worth approximately $100 million.

CHAPTER THIRTEEN

BASKETBALL

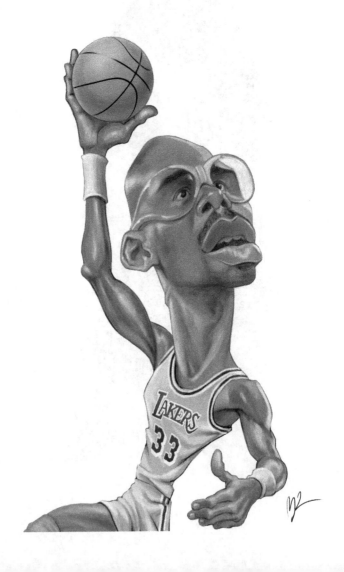

Kareem Abdul-Jabbar

Michael Jordan was an amazing talent and took the NBA to heights of popularity never before imagined. His highlight reels can entertain for hours and his charisma is nearly as bright as his basketball talent. Jordan also undoubtedly had the finest PR machine in the history of the sport. Having acknowledged all that, Kareem Abdul-Jabbar is the greatest basketball player in the history of the game. By literally any measure, Abdul-Jabbar was superior. His high school team, Power Memorial High School won 71 straight games as they dominated New York City high school hoops for three city championships. His college team, UCLA, won the NCAA Championship all three years that Abdul-Jabbar played varsity ball and he was named MVP of the NCAA tournament each of those three years. He was the first player chosen in the 1969 NBA Draft and took a Milwaukee Bucks expansion team from the cellar to NBA Champions in just his second year as a professional. He won the NBA Most Valuable Player (MVP) award three times in his first five years in the league.

Kareem may be best known for his years with the Los Angeles Lakers. Along with Magic Johnson he was an essential part of the "Showtime" teams that helped raise the both the NBA's profile and its dollar value to levels the league had never before known. He played 20 professional seasons in all and retired practically owning the NBA record book. He won the MVP award six times, he made the NBA All-Star squad a record nineteen times and was a fifteen time All-NBA choice. He won six NBA Championships as a player and was twice named the NBA Finals MVP. When he finished his final season in 1989 no player had ever scored more points, blocked more shots, won more Most Valuable Player Awards, played in more All-Star Games or logged more seasons than him. NBA coaching legend Pat Riley and all time basketball great Julius Erving have both called Kareem the greatest basketball player of all time. They are both correct.

Abdul-Jabbar is now widely acclaimed as a contributing columnist for newspapers and magazines around the world. In 2016 President Obama awarded him the Presidential Medal of Freedom.

James Naismith

There would be no debate about who the greatest basketball player of all time is if not for one man, James Naismith. Naismith invented the game in 1891 while teaching in Springfield, Massachusetts. He literally wrote the rule book (which in 2010 would sell at auction for more than $4.3 million). YMCAs helped quickly spread the popularity of basketball and by 1904 it was an Olympic demonstration sport.

After leaving Springfield, James Naismith earned his medical degree but was drawn back to his own creation. He became the University of Kansas Athletic Director in 1898 and founded their basketball program. He served as their first coach, launching what would become one of the most storied college basketball programs in the country. Ironically Naismith is the only University of Kansas men's basketball coach ever to have a losing record. Today more than three hundred million people play basketball worldwide. The annual NCAA Tournament generates more than $1 billion in revenue each year. The NBA has thirty teams and the average value for each team is $1.9 billion. At least twenty individual basketball players were slated to make more than $30 million for the 2020 NBA season. The game has come a long way from peach baskets nailed to the wall.

Naismith is universally recognized for his contribution. Springfield, Massachusetts is home to the Naismith Memorial Basketball Hall of Fame. The NCAA named its awards for both the best player and for the best coach after Naismith. Statues of the game's creator sit in his birth town of Almonte, Ontario, Canada, in Springfield and on the University of Kansas campus.

Jerry West

It's not uncommon to hear that an all time great in a professional sport exemplifies all the sport stands for. Extremely rare however, is for one player to literally be the face of a game. Jerry West is just that rare. The NBA logo is a field of blue and red evenly split by the white silhouette of a basketball player dribbling a ball. For the casual fan, the silhouette could be a generic image. In reality the logo figure is based on one of hoops' all time greats, Jerry West.

After leading West Virginia University to the 1959 NCAA championship game West was chosen as the second pick in the NBA draft by the Minneapolis Lakers. He played professional basketball from 1960 until 1974 and was elected to the NBA All-Star Team every year he played. Known as "Mr. Clutch" West holds the NBA record for the highest points per game average in a playoff series at 46.3 points per game.

Retiring from the hardwood was only the beginning for Jerry West however. He became Head Coach of the Lakers in 1976 and led them to the playoffs in all of his three seasons. After working as a scout, West became General Manager of the Lakers and is widely credited with assembling the Lakers dynasty team of the 1980s, which included five NBA Championships. Later in his career he went to the Golden State Warriors as an executive board member and earned two more NBA Championships. In 2017 he joined the Los Angeles Clippers. They have improved dramatically each season West has been with the team and at the time the 2019-2020 NBA season was suspended due to the coronavirus pandemic, the Clippers had the second best record in the league.

Larry Bird
Larry Legend, also know as the hick from French Lick, played thirteen seasons with the Boston Celtics of the NBA. He won the league's Most Valuable Player trophy three consecutive seasons, from 1984 through 1986 and his Celtics were a fixture season after season in the 1980s playoff picture. The Celtics won three NBA Championships in the era and Bird was NBA Finals MVP for two of those.

He first came to prominence at Indiana State University. He had three great years and led the Sycamores to the NCAA tournament for the first time in history in his final year. They were 33-0 entering the 1979 NCAA Championship game against Magic Johnson and Michigan State. Michigan State won the game 75–64. When he signed with the Boston Celtics Bird became the highest paid rookie in the history of professional sports. It was money well spent. In his first year

Bird scored 21.3 points per game and was named Rookie of the Year.

Larry Bird had the good fortune of playing with and against some of basketball's all time greats. In 1992, along with Magic Johnson and Michael Jordan, Bird anchored the men's U.S. Olympic basketball team, lovingly known as "The Dream Team." It is generally considered the greatest team since the creation of the sport.

Bird's winning ways continued even after his playing days were over. He coached the Indiana Pacers from 1997 to 2000. He was recognized as the NBA Coach of the Year following the 1997-1998 season. Bird later became President of Basketball Operations for the Pacers, a position he held until he retired for good in 2012.

CHAPTER FOURTEEN

— — —

FOOTBALL

Walter Payton

The Walter Payton NFL Man of the Year award is presented annually by the National Football League (NFL) honoring a player's volunteer and charity work, as well as his excellence on the field. What is most amazing about the award is that Walter Payton is remembered for being likable, giving and caring even more than he is remembered for his athletic grace. That is no small feat considering when Payton retired he held the league records for total career rushing yardage, most combined career yards from scrimmage, most seasons with 1,000 or more yards rushing (10), most yards gained in a single game, most games with 100 or more yards gained in a career (77), and most career touchdowns earned by rushing (110).

Payton's nickname was Sweetness. It described everything about him including his personality, his graceful play and his giving nature. The man was pure good. He was named to nine career Pro Bowls. In 1977 he won the league's Most Valuable Player award. In 1985 his Chicago Bears romped to a 15-1 season and a Super Bowl win. Hall of Fame NFL player and Bears coach Mike Ditka described Payton as the greatest football player he had ever seen but even greater as a human being.

Sadly his ability to contribute to society after his retirement was cut short. Payton died at aged 45 after suffering from a rare liver disease.

Tom Brady

Being labeled as the greatest of all time while still playing your sport every Sunday might seem like a daunting challenge. For Tom Brady however, it is an incentive to continue to excel well into his 40s. It's pretty hard to argue with the "greatest" tag. Brady has played in nine Super Bowls, won six of them and been the Super Bowl MVP a record four times. He has led his team to more division titles (17) than any other quarterback in NFL history. He is also the only quarterback to reach 200 regular season wins. The list of accomplishments goes on and on.

Brady has cultivated a reputation as a respectful, clean living guy. He credits his longevity in playing to a strict health regimen which includes meditation and yoga. According to *Men's Health*, 80 percent of the quarterback's diet is vegetables and he avoids starchy foods like bread and potatoes. He drinks at least 25 glasses of electrolyte-infused water a day.

Just in case being the best at his craft, earning money beyond the imagination and generally being the poster boy for all that is good wasn't enough, Brady married a Brazilian super-model. They have two children together. Reports that he has X-Ray vision and can fly have not been confirmed.

Roger Staubach
Roger Staubach was like a character straight out of central casting. He played college football for the U.S. Naval Academy. He was named All-American and won the 1963 Heisman Trophy as the best college player in football. After graduating from the Naval Academy he served four years in the U.S. Navy.

Because of his military service his professional football career didn't start until he was twenty seven years old, but Staubach certainly made up for lost time. He played with the Dallas Cowboys from 1969 to 1979 and led the Cowboys into the playoffs each of those years except one. He played in four Super Bowls, winning two. His squeaky clean image as the All American boy along with his ability to win games helped establish Dallas as America's Team.

Every football fan has heard of the "Hail Mary pass." That started with Roger Staubach in a 1975 playoff game. The Cowboys were losing with less than a minute to go when Staubach launched a 50-yard bomb. It was caught for a touchdown and an unlikely last minute victory. After the game the QB referred to it as a "Hail Mary" and the term has been repeated thousands of times by sportscasters ever since.

Staubach was inducted into the Pro Football Hall of Fame in 1985. He later received the Presidential Medal Presidential Medal of Freedom in 2018.

Joe Namath

If there was ever a professional athlete who epitomized "cool" it was Joe Namath. He guaranteed his heavy underdog New York Jets would win Super Bowl II and they did. He wore full-length fur coats on the sidelines. He loved to party, he loved the ladies and of course he loved football.

Namath was a three sport star in high school and fielded multiple offers from Major League Baseball teams but his family wanted him to go to college. Originally he planned to play football for Notre Dame but according to a Playboy magazine interview, he changed his mind after realizing there were no girls at the catholic school. Instead he played his college football at the University of Alabama under

coaching legend Bear Bryant. Bryant called Namath the
most natural athlete he had ever coached. When Namath
turned pro both the National Football League and the
American Football League (AFL) wanted him. He agreed to a
contract with the AFL's New Jersey Jets for a huge sum.

At one point near the peak of his popularity Namath posed
for a magazine advertisement wearing panty hose, showing
he was man enough to do pretty much anything. "Broadway
Joe" was inducted into the Pro Football Hall of Fame in
1985.

CHAPTER FIFTEEN

BASEBALL

Hank Aaron

How can a professional baseball player retire with more home runs, more extra base hits and more runs batted in than any player in history and still be underrated? Ask Hank Aaron. The likable, humble legend seldom generated the headlines that many flashier players did. Statistically however, Aaron has the most impressive resume since Abner Doubleday created the game. Some recognize his place atop baseball history crystal clearly. Muhammed Ali for example, once described Aaron as "The only man I idolize more than myself " Big words coming from the least humble man on the planet.

Hank was a rookie with the Milwaukee Braves in 1954. He made the All-Star team in 1955. He had the best batting average in the National League in 1956 and in 1957 he was the league MVP, leading the Braves to a World Series Championship in the process. For a kid who started out hitting bottle caps with broomsticks, hitting a baseball appeared to come easy. The U.S. Postal Service gave Aaron a plaque in 1973 as he was chasing baseball's home run record. It was in recognition of receiving more mail than any non-politician ever.

Aaron retired from the game in 1976 but hardly slowed down. The Hank Aaron Chasing the Dream Foundation has given thousands of scholarships to kids to pursue their life dreams. Aaron also donated $3 million to the Morehouse School of Medicine in Atlanta.

In 1999, Major League Baseball announced the introduction of the Hank Aaron Award to honor the best overall offensive performer in the American and National Leagues. Aaron has received the Presidential Citizens Medal and the Presidential Medal of Freedom.

Lou Gehrig

Lou Gehrig played first base for the New York Yankees from June of 1925 until early in the 1939 season. Gehrig had a career batting average of .340 and averaged 147 RBIs per season. To put that in perspective, no other Major League Baseball player reached 147 RBIs again for even a single season until 1977. He had 184 RBIs in the 1931 season, which stands as the single season American League record to this day. In 1934 he won baseball's Triple Crown, leading the American League in batting average (.363), home runs (49) and runs batted in (165). Adding to all that excellence, Gehrig played 2,130 consecutive games and earned the nickname Iron Horse. His consistency and durability became indelible stamps on his reputation.

After an uncharacteristically bad start to the 1939 season, Gehrig pulled himself out of the Yankees lineup in early May. In June of that same year, on Gehrig's 36th birthday, he was diagnosed with amyotrophic lateral sclerosis (ALS). The cruel disease attacks its victims with rapidly increasing paralysis, difficulty in swallowing and speaking, and a life expectancy of less than three years. Gehrig never played another game.

In 1939, after professional baseball waived the standard waiting period, Gehrig was elected to the Baseball Hall of Fame. He was also the first Major League player to have his uniform number retired by his team. Gehrig died June 2, 1941, less than two years after his diagnosis. Flags at ballparks all over America flew at half-mast in his honor.

Ted Williams

Virtually no one will argue with the fact that Ted Williams was among professional baseball's all time greats. He played professionally for the Boston Red Sox from 1939 through 1960, compiling a lifetime batting average of .344, including hitting .406 in the 1941 season. That would be the last time any Major League ballplayer hit above .400 for a full season. Williams was a nineteen-time All-Star, was twice named the American League (AL) MVP, won the AL batting title six times and twice won the Triple Crown.

What is up for debate however, is what kind of a guy Williams was. He feuded with the media throughout his career. Despite serving two separate tours of duty as a Navy flyer, once in World War II and once in the Korean War, the media questioned his character. Even when he won the Triple Crown, sports writers shunned Williams by choosing a different player as the league MVP. A bit of a curmudgeon, Williams refused to exercise the courtesy of tipping his cap, even to his adoring fans. In the "better late than never" category, on Ted Williams Day at Fenway Park in 1991, Williams pulled a Red Sox cap from inside his jacket and tipped it to the crowd. He was 72 years old.

Williams died in the summer of 2002 and left behind a will indicating he wished to be cremated. Two of his children however, had other plans. According to *Sports Illustrated*, after his death the Splendid Splinter's body was flown to the Alcor Life Extension Foundation in Scottsdale, Arizona. There he was surgically decapitated and his head and body are separately preserved cryogenically. His baseball reputation will live on forever and apparently some family members are in hopes Ted Williams himself will too.

George Brett

The Baseball Hall of Fame describes George Brett this way: For three decades, he was the standard by which other hitters were judged – seemingly mastering the art of hitting line drives. In 1980 baseball fans everywhere were riveted as Brett made a run at the magic .400 mark – a number that hadn't been reached since Ted Williams hit .406 in 1941. Brett kept his average over .400 deep into the summer, but ultimately had to settle for a season average of .390. The spectacular season earned him the AL Most Valuable Player Award.

In 1990 Brett won his third of three batting titles and in the process became the first and only player to win a batting title in three different decades. Two years later, he picked up his 3,000th career hit. He retired after 21 seasons with the Royals as one of only four players with 3,000 hits, 300 home runs and a .300 batting average. He was inducted into the Baseball Hall of Fame in 1999 on the first ballot.

Despite all his amazing statistics, Brett is best remembered by many fans for the infamous 1983 Pine Tar incident. The Royals were trailing the New York Yankees with two out in the top of the ninth inning. Brett came to the plate and hit a two run homer to put the Royals ahead. Yankee manager Billy Martin protested, complaining that the pine tar on Brett's bat exceeded league rules and the home run should be disallowed. The umpires spent what seemed like an eternity trying to determine the correct rule, ultimately agreeing with the Yankees manager. They declared Brett was out and the game was over with a Yankees victory. Brett was livid. He charged out of the dugout and had to be physically restrained from attacking the home plate umpire.

The oft forgotten post script to that story is that the Royals protested the outcome to the American League and as a result George Brett's home run was reinstated. Nearly a month later the game was picked up from the point of Brett's home run and completed.

The Royals won the game.

CHAPTER SIXTEEN
– – –
LEISURE &
ENTERTAINMENT

Chess

According to the 1913 book by Harold James Ruthven Murray that many current day chess historians consider to be the bible of the game, Chess originated in India around the 7th century. Murray was no casual observer either. He studied Latin and Arabic for the sole purpose of tracing the history and origins of chess.The languages helped him understand historical and archaeological manuscripts that he painstakingly tracked down as part of the research process. It took Murray seven years to complete his research before beginning to compile his nine hundred page publication.

During the Middle Ages, as Islam spread across the Middle East and in Europe, so did chess. Eventually the game made its way to such important ports of call as Britain and Germany, where its popularity exploded.

Today, the virtual nature of the world wide web has contributed to yet another spread in popularity. It is estimated there are eight hundred million chess players in the world. A quick look at chess.com shows fifteen million players registered on that site alone. Among that staggering number of eight hundred million players however, only about 1500 are considered grandmasters. Check mate.

Slot Machines

Humans have always found games of chance to be enticing. The gambling industry in the United States alone is worth $261 billion and employs 1.8 million people. Industry records indicate just under half of all gamblers play slot machines, making it the most popular form of gambling.

The first slot machine was created in 1887 by Charles Fey in San Francisco, California. It had three spinning wheels and had five symbols: horseshoes, diamonds, spades, hearts and a Liberty Bell. Three bells in a row produced the biggest payout and thus the game was known as Liberty Bell. It was wildly popular, both in the United States and abroad. Knock-off versions began to be made by a variety of manufacturers and popped up everywhere from saloons and brothels to bowling alleys and barber shops.

In 1963, Ballys developed the first fully electromechanical slot machine, allowing big action with virtually no help from a casino attendant. The first video slot machine was developed in 1976 and debuted on the floor of the Hilton Hotel in Las Vegas. Slot machines are the most lucrative form of casino gambling and make up more than 60% of the average casino's income.

The Jukebox
When many people think of the music jukebox they think of the 1950s era machines. The classic jukebox had buttons with letters and numbers on them that when entered in combination would play the song of the customers choice. It may surprise most people to know that the original jukebox was created all the way back in 1889.

Louis Glass and William S. Arnold put a coin operated machine made from an Edison cylinder phonograph into a San Francisco saloon. It cost a customer five cents to play the recording. There were no large speakers in those days so customers would listen through one of four listening tubes. In the first six months that original jukebox generated over $1000. That is a lot of nickels.

The first selective jukebox was introduced in 1927 by the Automated Musical Instrument Company. It allowed the listener to choose from multiple songs. During the World War II era, three out of every four records produced in America went into jukeboxes. They received the newest songs first and played music without the commercial interruptions of radio.

In a 2020 article from *ThoughtCo* called "History of the Jukebox" Mary Bellis explains how the 45 rpm vinyl record revolutionized the jukebox and was used for decades before giving way to CDs and eventually MP3s. Regardless of the source one thing is for certain, people love music and are willing to spend some of their hard earned money to hear their favorite songs.

Lego

The Lego Group began in the Denmark carpentry workshop of Ole Kirk Christiansen in 1932. Ole Kirk's shop started in the industry by making wooden toys such as piggy banks, pull toys, cars and trucks and houses. Their products were great but sales were not. The Great Depression made optional consumer items like toys a tough sell.

Lego purchased a plastic injection molding machine in 1947. The resulting initial modular toys were not exactly an immediate hit. Many customers preferred traditional wood or metal toys over this new substance called plastic. Lego hung in there, however. By 1960 they had dropped all wood toys and committed fully to the plastic products that could be assembled and disassembled over and over.

Corporate Lego says their name is an abbreviation of the two Danish words "leg godt", meaning "play well".

Apparently Lego has playing well down to a science. It was named Toy of the Century twice and despite all the 21st century online temptations and distractions that exist today, Lego continues to thrive in the toy market.

Crossword Puzzles

Shortly before Christmas in 1913 a journalist from Liverpool, England by the name of Arthur Wynne created the first crossword puzzle. It was in the shape of a diamond and had no internal black squares. It was printed in the Sunday edition of *New York World* and was an immediate hit. The crossword became a weekly feature.

CrosswordTournament.com says Crossword puzzles are the most popular and widespread word game in the world. For over 50 million people crossword puzzles are a part of their daily lives. Pop Quiz: What is the five letter first name of Bugs Bunny's fowl friend?

CHAPTER SEVENTEEN

FASHION

The Bikini

Much of the world was feeling happy, carefree and ready to cut loose in the immediate aftermath of World War II. A French engineer by the name of Louis Reard capitalized on that social attitude. In 1946 he introduced a small two piece women's bathing suit that he called the bikini. The name came from the Bikini Atoll where the United States had just begun testing the atomic bomb mere days before his announcement.

Micheline Bernardini, an exotic dancer at the Casino de Paris had no qualms about appearing nearly nude in public,. She modeled the new beach fashion at the unveiling. To say the publicity was effective would be a massive understatement. French women welcomed the design. Men loved it. The Catholic Church, some in the media and a majority of the public however, protested that the design was too risqué. Following her appearance in the bikini Bernardini received 50,000 fan letters. Thanks to Bernardini's look and the clever name, the bikini was a definite hit.

Sunglasses

Sunglasses as we know them today were invented in 1929 by Sam Foster. Initially popularized by movie stars and celebrities of the era, Foster mass produced inexpensive sunglasses, appropriately enough made from celluloid. He marketed his shades under the brand name Foster Grant and launched sales on the beaches of Atlantic City, New Jersey. It didn't take long for sunglasses to take off nationwide. Life magazine reported that twenty million pair were sold in the United States in 1937 and that 75% of those sales were strictly for fashion purposes.

Bausch & Lomb perfected a special dark-green tint that absorbed light in the yellow band of the spectrum in the 1930s in research done at the request of Army Air Corps. They were used to protect pilots from high altitude glare.

Clever marketing campaigns in the 1960s and 1970s pushed sunglass sales into the stratosphere. Fashion designers began to market eyewear under their own brand names. Hollywood made shades very trendy. JFK, The Blues Brothers, Tom Cruise, Don Johnson, Bono and Lady Gaga are all stars that have made sunglasses the ultimate cool fashion accessory.

Denim Jeans
Denim jeans offer the perfect combination of cool and comfort. Originally designed as a work pant, jeans became the rebellious choice of youth in the 1950s thanks in great part to the films of Marlon Brando and James Dean. Today they are arguably the most common and most popular trouser on the planet.

Denim jeans were invented by Jacob Davis and Levi Strauss in 1873. Davis was a tailor who frequently bought fabric from Strauss. In 1872 he asked Strauss to partner with him on a work pant reinforced with copper rivets. They experimented with different fabrics before finally settling on denim. The name Levi's would go on to become synonymous with denim jeans.

Today there are brands like Wrangler selling from Walmart for under $20 per pair and designer brand jeans selling in excess of $300. On average a pair of denim jeans in the

United States costs about $60. Americans spend over $38 million on denim pants every single day. For the mathematically challenged that comes out to about $14 billion in annual sales.

The Zipper

Perhaps the most under appreciated invention in fashion is the zipper. Its origins date back to 1851 when Elias Howe patented the Automatic Continuous Clothing Closure. Similar to the modern day zipper, Howe's creation was pulled shut with string. Neither the name nor his patented invention took off.

The modern zipper became a reality in 1917 when Gideon Sundback, a Swedish-American electrical engineer, who had married the plant manager's daughter at the Fastener Manufacturing and Machine Company, created what he called a Separable Fastener. He licensed it to the Goodrich Company for use on their galoshes. Goodrich decided "zipper" was easier to say than separable fastener and the name stuck.

In the 1930s sales of children's clothing with zippers really took off. A marketing campaign promoted the fact zippers would allow children to dress themselves. Moms everywhere loved it. Some years later NASA worked with the zipper industry to create airtight zippers for use on high altitude suits and eventually in space suits. Today the most popular brand of zipper is YKK. Each year they produce the equivalent of 1.2 million miles of zipper.

Sneakers

In the 1970s Red Ball Keds were the pinnacle of trendy in footwear if you were eight years old. Keds got their start much, much earlier however. In 1892 the U.S. Rubber Company came up with comfortable rubber shoes with canvas tops and called them Keds. Also in 1892 Marquis Converse produced the first shoe made just for basketball. They were called Converse All-Stars. They were the first high top. The name sneaker quickly took hold because the shoes were so quiet someone wearing a pair could sneak up on you.

In 1923, an Indiana hoops star named Chuck Taylor endorsed the Converse shoes, and they became known as Chuck Taylor All-Stars. It was the first of what would prove to be a very lucrative partnership between athletes and sneaker makers. Chuck Taylor All-Stars are the best-selling basketball shoes of all time. As with most commercial enterprises, sneaker branding and exposure are essential to success. German Adi Dassler created a sneaker named after himself called Adidas. The brand became immensely popular worldwide. In 1936 US track star Jesse Owens wore Adidas when he won four gold medals.

Sales of sneakers escalated to a whole different level after 1984. That was the year Michael Jordan teamed up with Nike to make Air Jordans, the most popular sneaker ever made. Its success led the industry to go wild with color and design. It also led to a more scientific sports shoe, enhancing performance and protecting the athlete. Eventually all major sneaker manufacturers began to make specialty sneakers for nearly every sport. Unique designs were made for cross training, running, basketball and tennis.

Sneakers account for more than $55 billion in annual sales worldwide. According to Forbes magazine, Michael Jordan branded sneakers account for $2.6 billion of that every year in the United States alone.

CHAPTER EIGHTEEN

MEDICINE

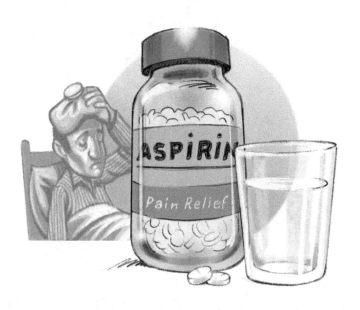

Soap

Cleanliness is next to Godliness so the saying goes. Whether that is true or not, cleanliness may at least delay you meeting the almighty one. By killing germs and bacteria before they become an issue, potentially fatal illnesses can be stopped before they even take root.

Available evidence suggests the first soap-like material was developed around 2800 BC and was used for cleaning cooking utensils or goods and also was used for medicinal purposes. Early Egyptians, Babylonians and others in the region mixed fat, oils and salts to get their version of soap.

Common soap bars were invented in the 19th century and commercial soap as we know it today gained common acceptance during World War I. German scientists mixed together various synthetic compounds and these detergents were used as cleaning agents during the war. Cleaning wounds thoroughly saved countless lives.

Much of the good work soap does to save lives today is preventative. Perfectly healthy people may have been exposed to harmful circumstances and never even know, simply because of the great medicinal value of soap. Some would tell you soap has saved more lives than penicillin and thus is the most significant breakthrough in medical history.

Penicillin

Most know the discovery of penicillin, one of the world's first antibiotics, was a turning point in medicine. It gave doctors a tool that could literally cure their patients of many deadly infectious diseases. What most don't know is that penicillin was discovered by accident.

Scottish bacteriologist Alexander Fleming was conducting research in 1928 using petri dishes of bacteria cultures. He left one of the cultures uncovered for several days by mistake. When he discovered his error he noticed a green mold has started to grow and was killing some of the bacteria he had been cultivating. The specific mold was identified as penicillium notatum. Fleming began further experiments in earnest and by 1929 he introduced penicillin to the world and demonstrated it could cure bacterial infections.

Penicillin became the go-to medicine of choice to fight staph and strep infections among other ailments. It went into widespread use in 1942 and continues to be prescribed today.

Pasteurization
French scientist Louis Pasteur first demonstrated in the 1860s that abnormal fermentation of wine and beer could be prevented by heating the beverages for a few minutes. The heat treatment process destroyed pathogenic microorganisms in many food and beverage items. The process allowed people to store consumables longer without spoiling and in turn, made those foods safer to eat or drink. For centuries milk borne illnesses including tuberculosis, salmonella and typhoid fever killed millions of people every year. No more. Nowadays nearly every liquid sold in stores is pasteurized. Due to its organic and nutrient rich nature, milk is one of the most susceptible liquids to this process and only pasteurized milk is considered safe by the United States FDA. Even as recently as the early 20th century, cow milk was responsible for approximately one quarter of all food borne illnesses. Fast forward to present

time and you'll find that on average, only three people die each year in the United States from milk-related sickness. This is due almost entirely to pasteurization.

Pasteur is also credited with the development of the first vaccines for rabies and anthrax.

Insulin
Prior to the discovery of insulin in 1921, diabetes was essentially a death sentence. Doctors could put patients on strict diets which would sometimes extend a patient's life expectancy but by and large there was very little else medical experts could do for them. Only when research went to the dogs did the tables began to turn.

In 1889, two German researchers found that when the pancreas gland was removed from dogs, the animals developed symptoms of diabetes and died soon afterward. Additional research narrowed the details of their discovery down considerably and found just one specific chemical was missing from the pancreas in humans with diabetes. We know this chemical as insulin.

In 1921, a young doctor named Frederick Banting figured out how to remove a thick brown muck from a dog's pancreas. That muck was insulin. In early experiments Banting was able to keep a severely diabetic dog alive with regular treatments using the insulin. The dog stayed alive as long as there was a supply. 70 days later he died when the insulin ran out and Banting could no longer treat him. Banting and his research team honed their product even further and made a more refined version from the pancreas of cows.

Early in 1922 a fourteen year old Canadian boy who was dying from diabetes became the first human being injected with Banting's insulin. Within 24 hours, the boy's dangerously high blood glucose levels dropped to near-normal levels. Word of the success spread quickly and by 1923 Frederick Banting and one of his team members, John Macleod, had been awarded the Nobel Prize in Medicine. Medical giant Eli Lilly got involved and soon had produced enough insulin to supply all of North America.

Oral Contraceptives

For centuries virtue was given as the primary reason to avoid sex outside of marriage. In many cultures the consequences of a pregnancy out of wedlock were dire. The threat of those consequences were enough to discourage many young women from tempting fate or their boyfriend. Famed feminist activist Margaret Sanger openly dreamed of the day in which women did not have to worry about pregnancy nor its myriad of complications. She helped launch the first serious research into oral contraceptives.

The first effective and efficient birth control pill was developed by a team that included a man of Asian descent and a couple of white guys. Gregory Pincus headed the project. He and Min-Chueh Chang were responsible for the basic concept of the pill. John Rock conducted the actual clinical trials. Once approved by the FDA, the pill was initially prescribed only to married women. It was later made available to all women regardless of relationship status. The Pope is still not thrilled by the breakthrough but couples everywhere have been ecstatic.

The pill is often the target of those trying to pinpoint the primary cause of moral decay in western civilization. Critics say the oral contraceptive's popularity has contributed to an increase in casual sex, unmarried couples living together, swinger couples and the glorification of recreational sex by the entertainment industry.

Vitamins
Famed sailor Christopher Columbus is the subject of many legendary tales. One such story centers around some of his crew suffering the ill effects of scurvy. Sailors of the day typically had a bland and limited diet for months at a time while at sea and it was not uncommon they would come down with a variety of physical ailments caused by the onset of scurvy. Many sailors died as a result of the disease. Legend has it that on one particular journey Columbus had several sailors suffering from the dreaded disease. Rather than die on board ship, they asked their Captain if he would drop them off on an island to die peacefully. Several months later Columbus and his remaining crew again passed the same island on their return trip. They were greeted by shouts of joy and waves from the shore line. It seems the men, long assumed dead by Columbus, had been enjoying the abundant fruit life on the island and their scurvy had subsided. We now know the restoration of Vitamin C to their diet is what saved the men.

Despite the anecdotal story, it wasn't until 1905 an Englishmen named William Fletcher became the first scientist to determine that the removal of certain factors from food can lead to diseases. These factors are called vitamins.

Early in the 20th century Elmer V. McCollum and Marguerite Davis discovered Vitamin A. Vitamin B was also discovered by Elmer V. McCollum about 2 years later. Vitamin C was the first vitamin to be artificially synthesized in 1935. In 1922, Edward Mellanby discovered Vitamin D while researching a disease called rickets.

Today doctors aren't the only ones who understand the value of vitamins. Marketers do too. Vitamin and nutritional supplement production reached nearly $31 billion in sales in 2018 in the United States.

Organ Transplants

The practice of organ transplants is one of the most complex areas of modern medicine. Swiss Doctor Theodor Kocher performed the first successful organ tissue transplant in 1883. He found that transplanting a portion of healthy thyroid tissue to a troubled thyroid gland stopped it from causing goiter yet allowed the organ to continue to provide a base level of thyroid hormone to the body. Kocher's success became the blueprint for the transplant of other types of organ tissue, including the pancreas and the kidney.

A kidney was the first full organ to be transplanted successfully. That happened in 1954 at Boston's Peter Bent Brigham Hospital. The surgery had a bit of an asterisk noted beside it in the history books however. The donor was 23-year-old Ronald Herrick and the recipient was his twin brother Richard. Donor and recipient were genetically identical, making the transplant process somewhat easier.

British immunologist Peter Medawar received the 1960 Nobel Prize for his discovery of acquired immune tolerance. It was through his work that anti-rejection drugs made it possible for patients to receive organs from non-identical donors. In the decade that followed liver, heart and pancreas transplants saw some success. One of the less successful experimental surgeries involved the transplant of kidneys from chimpanzees into human patients. Suffice to say it didn't go well.

The first successful human heart transplant was performed by the South African surgeon Christiaan Barnard in December of 1967. Eventually as transplants became more common it became apparent guidelines and clearinghouse information were necessary. The U.S. Congress passed the National Organ Transplant Act in 1984 in order to allocate available organs and collect data about transplant candidates, recipients and donors.

The Respirator
Breathe Easy was a small oxygen supply company that operated in New England for many years. Those two words have also been the goal of virtually every human being since the dawn of mankind. In the 16th century Leonardo da Vinci recommended the use of a wet woven cloth to protect against the pollution caused by the warfare of the day. It wasn't until the 20th century however, that humans began to harness mechanical devices to make breathing easier.

The Iron Lung was unveiled in 1927 by two medical researchers from Harvard. Philip Drinker and Louis Agassiz Shaw used an iron box and two vacuum cleaners to create a push-pull motion on a person's chest. As the polio epidemic gripped America, hospitals lined up units of the Iron Lung to assist those afflicted with the dreaded disease.

In the 1950s and 1960s Dr. Forrest Bird developed some of the first portable ventilators for people with chronic heart and/or lung disease. The fact his creations were relatively small, easily transported and extremely reliable meant they were rapidly accepted for both hospital and in-home care. In 2020 the world saw demand for life-saving ventilators spike again when the global coronavirus pandemic struck.

Aspirin
When you have a headache or a fever your first thought is probably not to get the bark of a willow tree. More likely it is to take a couple of aspirin. Most don't realize that one is derived from the other. In 1894 a young chemist named Felix Hoffman took a job with the Bayer pharmaceutical group. Three years of lab work later Hoffman successfully synthesized acetylsalicylic acid. Bayer formally named the concoction Aspirin. Hoffman was recognized as the inventor of the elixir on the U.S. patent. One key ingredient? A chemical found in the bark of the willow tree. By 1899 Bayer was selling Aspirin worldwide.

The science behind aspirin's success as an analgesic, an anti-inflammatory and as an overall wonder drug wasn't really understood at the time of its creation. It wasn't until the 1960s and the 1970s that a British pharmacologist by the name of John Robert Vane was able to quantify how aspirin produces pain-relief and anti-inflammatory effects. His work led to new treatments for heart disease. It isn't an exaggeration to say his work has prevented countless heart attacks and strokes. He was awarded the Nobel Prize in Medicine in 1982.

Today Bayer Aspirin is the headliner among many Bayer owned health related products including Alka Seltzer and the Flintstones brand of vitamins.

MRI

Many necessary tools of medicine have unpleasant side effects or certain risks that come with their use. Magnetic resonance imaging (MRI) does just the opposite. It is a method of looking inside the body without using invasive surgery, nauseating dyes or radioactive X-rays. An MRI can show differences between healthy and unhealthy tissue. MRI can be used to examine the human brain, spine, abdomen, breasts, pelvic region, various joints, heart, blood vessels and more.

The MRI was invented by physician Raymond Vahan Damadian. His research led him to propose the concept of a medical device that could see layer by layer images of the human body and help in making an accurate diagnosis of a malady or injury. After a multi-year exhaustive development process, he was granted a patent in 1974. The first MRI equipment in healthcare facilities became available at the beginning of the 1980s. Only a dozen years later approximately 22,000 MRI cameras were in use worldwide, and more than 60 million MRI examinations were performed. Most medical experts describe the MRI as one of the most useful diagnostic tools in modern medicine.

If you've ever had an MRI and received the bill thereafter, you know it is expensive. The reason? The cost of the machine itself. A new MRI system costs around $1.2 million. High end systems can even approach a $3 million price tag. In June of 2020 it was announced that MRI will be used to detect brain injuries in football players. If the NFL closes up shop at some future point, you may have to point a finger at the MRI's recognition of brain injuries. Or perhaps blame Colin Kaepernick. It will likely be one or the other.

CHAPTER NINETEEN

WHITE GUYS YOU DON'T KNOW THAT YOU KNOW

Reed Hastings

Reed Hastings isn't exactly a household name. Certainly not like Walt Disney or Thomas Edison, yet during the COVID-19 outbreak of 2020 he was probably just as important to you as either of them. Reed Hastings is the co-founder, chairman and CEO of Netflix. He founded the company in 1995 as a DVD subscription service. In 2007 Netflix jumped ahead of the pack and began streaming content. Today they offer TV shows, movies and an ever increasing amount of original programming. According to the New York Times they have more than 150 million customers worldwide.

Hastings may be the only multi-billionaire that served two years in the Peace Corps. His original idea for a subscription based movie rental service came to him when he was six weeks late on returning a VHS tape to the store. They told him he owed $40. The same day he went to the gym and realized he was paying less for a monthly membership there than he had paid for the one video rental. Presto! Netflix was born. What started out with seven day rentals soon shifted over to unlimited DVDs for one monthly fee. In early 2007 Netflix shipped its one billionth DVD. Hastings wanted more. He saw a future where people could choose whatever they wanted to watch, whenever they wanted to watch it.

Today more than sixty million American homes stream their video content and a majority of those are Netflix subscribers. The impact Netflix has achieved became apparent when "Netflix and Chill" became part of the pop culture lexicon. It all happened because Reed Hasting was late returning an *Apollo 13* video to the rental store back in the 1990s.

James Watson, Francis Crick and Maurice Wilkins

James Watson, Francis Crick and Maurice Wilkins are three names that you may have never heard of, yet their work impacts the lives of virtually every living being. Watson, Crick and Wilkins are responsible for the discovery of DNA. You may remember the double helix model from your high school science text book. Watson and Crick came up with that. In fact, they were awarded the Nobel Prize for it in 1965. Officially the prize was "for their discoveries concerning the molecular structure of nucleic acids and its significance for information transfer in living material." It was the Swiss doctor, Maurice Wilkins however, working in a small laboratory in Germany, that took molecular structure to the next level, specifically discovering DNA.

Every human shares the same DNA. 99.9 percent the same DNA anyway. That tiny sliver of difference is what makes us all unique. Being shorter or taller, a person's skin tone or someone's predisposition to certain health maladies can all be studied through DNA.

Our differences in DNA are used in a variety of ways. Among humans it helps us get an in depth look at genetics for issues as complex as health problems or as simple as determining paternity. It is used in forensic science to determine or rule out crime suspects. DNA among other living creatures can be used for cloning. It can be used to assist in the correct labeling of food products. DNA is an essential element in the controversial practice of agricultura genetic modifications, a process intended to make it easier for farmers to produce more crops.

Robert Gallo, MD

In the 1980s a health scare spread across America and around the globe. HIV/AIDS, a slow-acting virus that attacks the immune system over an extended period, was spreading at an ever increasing rate. It was soon discovered that it could be spread through sexual contact, needle sharing among drug addicts, and blood products. Most thought a diagnosis of AIDS was a death sentence.

Robert Gallo is the scientist who co-discovered HIV as the cause of AIDS in 1984. His work included the development of the HIV blood test and research that led to HIV therapies to prolong the lives of those who had been infected. Dr. Gallo also discovered that a natural compound known as chemokines can block HIV and halt the progression of AIDS.

Gallo was part of a team that founded the Institute of Human Virology (IHV), which was awarded a $15 million grant from the Bill and Melinda Gates Foundation for its research into preventative HIV vaccines. Today IHV's patient base includes approximately 6,000 in Baltimore and Washington, D.C., and more than 1.3 million in African and Caribbean nations.

Dr. Gallo's work has been celebrated worldwide. He holds thirty five honorary doctorates and earned election into the National Academy of Sciences and the Institute of Medicine.

Jack Dorsey

Are you frustrated by President Trump's predilection to communicate via tweets? Blame Jack Dorsey. Dorsey is the co-founder and CEO of Twitter. He's not exactly your stereotypical CEO however. He sports a full sleeve tattoo and prior to accepting the title of Twitter's CEO he wore a nose ring. Don't go and get all judgmental based on his appearance though. In 2016 the unconventional leader gave one third of his Twitter stock to employees and in 2020 he promised to give away $1 billion of his own money to COVID-19 relief and related causes.

Fellow tech legends Bill Gates, Steve Jobs and Mark Zuckerberg all dropped out of college before completing their degree. Jack Dorsey did them one better. He dropped out of college twice. Like his counterparts Dorsey's imagination, ingenuity and know-how changed the world and brought him a fortune. On March 21, 2006, Jack Dorsey posted the world's first tweet. By 2010, Twitter had more than one hundred five million users who collectively tweeted fifty five million times a day. Today Twitter has more than three hundred thirty million global monthly active users.

In 2009 Dorsey also co-founded Square, the simple and convenient credit card payment mobile device. He and his partner took Square public in 2015, adding even more to his tech generated fortune. By the way, although Dorsey created the Twitter platform that President Trump has used to raise the blood pressure of people all over the world, he may also be able to help you relax. Prior to his success in tech, Dorsey was a certified massage therapist.

CHAPTER TWENTY

— — —

GREAT
INVENTIONS

The Wheel
Though often thought of as one of the earliest inventions, the wheel is a relative newcomer compared with agriculture, boats, cloth and pottery. Wheels first began to roll about 5000 years ago in what we now know as Iraq. They were initially used by potters to help shape clay. Later they were used for moving things around. Chariots were the first common mode of transportation to use the wheel.

Today the wheel is used for nearly every type of transportation including motorcycles, automobiles, trucks, trains and planes. All of these forms of transportation transformed our planet earth into one global community that can travel long distances in relatively short periods of time. The wheel has made it possible for mankind to exchange products and cultures with ease. It also has been an essential element in a potpourri of human creations ranging from the Wheel of Death to the Wheel of Fortune.

For a little perspective on the impact of the invention of the wheel, one look no further than the latest sales records. Overall tire shipments in the United States for the year 2019 were about three hundred thirty three million units. That is roughly one wheel for every American man, woman and child.

Beer
The Germans will tell you they make the greatest beer on earth. The Irish will make a similar claim. America's Budweiser has proclaimed itself the King of Beers. The debate about the best beer is likely to rage on for all eternity and is a great discussion to have, well... over a beer. One

question that can be addressed with less controversy is what the origins of the delightful libation were.

Beer experts will tell you that beer is the oldest recipe in the world. The first barley beer has been traced to records from ancient Egypt. In the ultimate archaeological find, papyrus rolls from around 5000 BC stipulate their beer was made with dates, pomegranates and a variety of herbs. It is believed the addition of barley to the blend actually originated in Iran.

If you have ever visited a fraternity house the day after a keg party you may have found lots of cups and glasses that still had remnants of beer stuck to the bottom. Archaeologists made a similar discovery in ceramic mugs from 3400 BC. The mugs still had sticky beer residue inside. Who was in charge of clean up in those days?

The first documented use of hops in beer is from the 9th century. In the ensuing centuries, Christian monks were among those that developed the hops seasoned brew into what we now think of as traditional beer. In 2020 the art of beer making is more popular than ever. There are roughly 7,000 breweries in the United States and according to the book *Neighborhood Change, One Pint at a Time*, roughly 4,000 of those are craft breweries. Those craft breweries employ more than 100,000 people and please the taste buds of men and women everywhere.

The Printing Press
For approximately 1400 years after Christ walked the earth, every manuscript was handwritten. Dipping a pen in ink enough times to perfectly produce an entire book was

cumbersome and time consuming. As a result books were expensive and sparse in number. In the twelfth and thirteenth century a very rudimentary form of printing came along in the form of letters cut on blocks of wood, dipped in ink and pressed to paper. It too was a slow, laborious process. Then came Johannes Gutenberg.

Gutenberg was a blacksmith, goldsmith, gem cutter and aspiring inventor. He arranged financing to develop several creative concepts he had. None panned out until one day he hit the jackpot. His prior employment had given him some experience working at a mint. Gutenberg theorized that if he could use cut blocks in stamping machinery he could make the printing process a lot faster. He chose to use metal blocks rather than wood and designed them so that they could easily be moved around to create any combination of words and sentences.

Johannes Gutenberg demonstrated his first working printing press publicly in 1450. Forty two lines could be printed simultaneously. This meant a significant drop in both the amount of labor and the cost of creating a book. Suddenly the ability to share knowledge was practical and affordable. The printing press literally changed the world.

Today digital presses make low-volume printing more affordable than ever. They require no plates or hands-on tinkering. Instead they use computerized laser jet technology to create printed materials quickly and efficiently.

Vaccination

According to the World Health Organization (WHO) medical records indicate that smallpox killed about 400,000 people in Europe on average most years during the 18th century. That changed, as did the way the world dealt with disease, in 1796 when British physician Edward Jenner immunized an eight year old boy. Jenner used a vaccinia virus and through further experimentation was able to release an official vaccine for smallpox in 1798. It was the first vaccine that proved to be both effective and long-lasting.

Thanks to the methods employed by Dr. Jenner, today we have no more polio, tetanus or rubella to speak of and kids everywhere can avoid the measles, mumps and other once common diseases by simply getting a shot.

Air Conditioning

In the year 1900 the population of the State of Florida was a little more than one half million people. Today Florida's population is in the range of 22 million. The primary reason for that amazing growth? An invention called air conditioning.

Some of the earliest attempts at cooling the temperature took place in 19th century Florida. John Gorrie was a physician who treated yellow fever patients. Keeping his sick patients cool and comfortable became his obsession and by 1851 he had patented his "cold air machine" in the United States. It used compressed air and water. It was a start, but had decidedly mixed results. For his efforts Dr. Gorrie is considered by some as the father of air conditioning and refrigeration.

More than fifty years later Willis Carrier, an engineer by trade, designed a system that included chilled coils. His machine could maintain a constant humidity level of 55 percent. The first model provided comfort to the workers of an industrial plant. It would have taken 108,000 pounds of ice every day to keep the plant as cool as his creation could.

Large manufacturers such as plants and mills installed this new form of air conditioning almost immediately. In 1914 a Minneapolis millionaire hired Willis Carrier to air condition his mansion. While Minnesota may not seem like the most likely place to launch air conditioning, that project opened the door to private home A/C units becoming a reality. In the 1920s Carrier installed air conditioning in more than 300 movie theaters throughout America. Ticket sales skyrocketed as a result and the summer movie blockbuster was born.

Today 89% of American homes have some form of air conditioning. According to U.S. government statistics air conditioners use about 6% of all the electricity produced in the United States.

The Internal Combustion Engine

For the better part of a century the steam engine was used as the primary source of energy, powering everything from factories to railway engines. In the mid-nineteenth century however, a German engineer name Nikolaus Otto came up with the first four-stroke internal combustion engine. In 1864 he created the world's first company focused entirely on internal combustion engines. It was time well spent. Otto was awarded the Gold Medal at the 1867 World Exhibition in Paris.

Otto's early efforts were not particularly practical, but were enormously important. They laid the ground work for the practical engines yet to come. By 1876 Otto and his partner created the first internal combustion engine that compressed the fuel mixture prior to combustion. The result was a remarkably higher efficiency than anything else of the era.

The Automobile

The Automotive Hall of Fame recognizes German Karl Benz as the inventor of the gas powered automobile. He created his first model in 1885 and patented it in 1886. He spent two more years perfecting his invention and in 1888 took home the highest award from the Munich Engineering Exposition. When he offered test rides to the public, Benz drew huge crowds.

Mercedes-Benz would go on to become recognized for producing one of the finest quality automobile lines in the world. Ford, General Motors and Dodge all launched early in the 20th century and became mainstays in the industry. In the early years moving people from point A to point B was the simple goal of every motor vehicle. Today innovation has lead to high tech headlamps, smart keys, rear-view back up cameras and GPS navigation in many models. Stereos and color schemes are essential elements in modern auto sales.

In 2018 approximately 5.3 million passenger cars were sold in the United States. Globally, automobile sales numbered around 79 million.

The Microphone
The late 19th century was an amazing time for innovation. The number of modern inventions that came to fruition in this period is staggering. Many items had fierce competition for who would cross the finish line first and be recognized as the inventor and awarded the patent. Such was the case with the microphone.

Emile Berliner was working with Thomas Edison in 1876. He filed the necessary paperwork with the United States government to patent a microphone transmitter. At approximately the same time, Alexander Graham Bell registered his magneto receiver. The patent office was unsure what to do because of the marked similarities between the two inventions. The fight for recognition and ownership went on for years. Finally in 1891 the Supreme Court recognized Berliner as the inventor of the microphone.

Ironically, although they had been adversaries in court, Bell Telephone company hired Berliner as their chief engineer and paid him $50,000 for his rights to the patent so they could market it. Berliner would go on to assist Alexander Graham Bell in the development and improvement of the telephone in the years thereafter.

The Refrigerator
Refrigeration is arguably the most important food storage invention ever. Lower temperatures slow bacteria from reproducing, thus delaying food from spoiling. A refrigerator maintains temperature at just a few degrees above freezing. The earliest versions of the modern refrigerator can be traced back to the early 1800s but it wasn't until after America's Civil War that German Carl von Linden invented

the first air separation and gas liquefaction processes. His invention made stable, reliable temperatures a reality.

American Fred W. Wolf created refrigerators for individual homes in 1913 and the next year the first practical electric refrigeration unit was introduced by another American, Nathaniel B. Wales. In the years and decades thereafter a variety of additional features were developed including adjustable shelves, auto-defrost and ice dispensers.

Freezers are similar units but they maintain the temperature below water's freezing point. They allow people to buy food in bulk and eat it at their leisure. Costco and Sam's Club are both very appreciative. At one time ice cream, one of America's favorite sweet treats, could only be purchased and eaten by going to where it was made and eating it on the spot. Thanks to reliable family freezers ice cream has become a staple in most American homes.

Sliced Bread
This is the invention by which all other inventions are measured. "It's the greatest thing since sliced bread" is a phrase woven into the American lexicon to indicate total approval. Otto Frederick Rohwedder created the first bread-slicing machine in Davenport, Iowa. This great idea however, disappeared for more than fifteen years and was nearly lost forever.

It seems Rohwedder came up with the design for a machine to cut an entire loaf of bread all at once in 1912, but his original prototype and the blueprints for his idea were lost in a fire. Apparently Rohwedder was busy because he didn't return to the idea for many years. He made his next model

in 1928. The first commercially successful consumer sliced bread was brought to market in 1930 by Wonder Bread. By 1933 80% of all bread made in America was pre-sliced with Rohwedder's invention. Think about that the next time you sit down to lunch with a sandwich.

Frozen Foods

While working as a fur trader in New Foundland, Canada, an American entrepreneur named Clarence Birdseye noticed that the fish he and the natives caught froze almost immediately after being pulled from the water. He further took note that the fish seemed just as tasty and fresh when later thawed and cooked as if they had just been fresh caught. According the United States Library of Congress Birdseye took these observations and theorized that quick freezing could save the freshness, maintain the nutrient value and could extend the usable life of food.

As an avid hunter, Birdseye was familiar with various methods of preserving food including salting and drying. He began to pay particular attention to freezing. When something was frozen slowly he noticed that the resulting ice crystals were large. Both the taste and texture of meat was compromised. Quick freezing however, had small ice crystals and very little damage to the meat or vegetables.

Birdseye returned to the United States and convinced an ice cream company to let him use their plant to tinker with his idea of freezing food. The year was 1924. It didn't take long for him to prove his theory. In 1927 he froze 1.6 million pounds of seafood. 1928 saw the first retail store freezer and in the years that followed, Birdseye consistently grew the industry. After World War II frozen food sales really took off and by the 1960s it was a $50 billion a year industry in the United States and $300 billion worldwide.

Miniature Golf

Golf is a challenging game that even some of the world's best athletes can't master. Miniature golf however, is a game that provides equal fun for a small child, the elderly or two teens on their first date.

Garnett Carter patented the game in 1927 under the name of "Tom Thumb Golf." He built a miniature golf course in the mountains of Tennessee in hopes of generating more customers to his hotel. He and his wife designed several obstacles and tricks into their course, utilizing a fairy theme. The obstacles became par for the course in miniature golf. It became so popular that Carter was quite sure he could replicate the success almost anywhere. The Carters founded the Fairyland Manufacturing Corporation and by 1930 had sold over 3000 Tom Thumb miniature golf franchises.

Dynamite
Here is a strange twist of fate. Man creates an explosive that mixes nitroglycerin with some stabilizing agents. Man earns fortune. Upon his death man leaves said fortune to honor those who have most advanced the cause of peace. Thus is the story of dynamite.

Alfred Nobel was a Swedish chemist and engineer. His family worked in the construction of buildings and bridges. Nobel's work inspired his quest to find something more effective and more controllable than black powder for blasting rock. The result? In 1867 Nobel created dynamite. Mining companies, construction companies and even the military all placed huge orders for the stable explosive. Nobel made a fortune in the truest sense of the word. Best estimates put his worth at the time of his death at $200 million.

Prior to his death Alfred Nobel set aside the vast bulk of his wealth to establish the Nobel Prizes. The initial categories he established reflected his own passions: physics, chemistry, physiology and literature. Probably the best known is the Nobel Peace Prize.

The Bar Code

In 1992 The New York Times reported that President George Bush had been mystified and amazed by bar code scanning equipment at a National Grocers Association meeting in Orlando, Florida. Their story made it seem that Bush was not familiar with this relatively new technology, and thus out of touch with the average American. As it turned out the New York Times article was more than a little misleading about the President's reaction. For those paying attention it also turned out that bar code technology wasn't really that new.The barcode was invented in 1951 by Joe Woodland. He came up with the concept while sitting on Miami Beach and drew his initial mental images of the concept in the sand. The invention was based on a visual version of Morse Code, represented by thick and thin bars. He was granted the patent on his idea of bar codes in 1952 but their practicality was questionable until 1960 when the laser was invented.

It wasn't until 1974 that the first commercial use of bar codes began. The first Universal Product Code (UPC) was scanned at a small Ohio supermarket. The use of bar codes really took off in the 1980s, particularly at grocery and retail outlets. It allowed giants like Walmart to instantly price items without applying individual price tags and more importantly, became a valuable tool in inventory control.

Cat Litter

Cat lovers everywhere need to say a prayer of thanks to Edward Lowe. In 1947 Lowe began selling a type of absorbent clay for the purpose of minimizing the odor and mess that came with owning an indoor cat. Prior to Lowe's eureka moment, most folks used either ash or sand for their cat's bathroom functions. The ash was messy and both smelled to high heaven.

Lowe's discovery was quite by accident. His Michigan family business sold a variety of goods including ice, sand, sawdust and kiln-dried clay. The clay was primarily used for absorbing grease spills. One day while Edward was working, a neighbor asked for some sand for her litter box. The sand was frozen so he gave her some of the granulated clay instead. She came back days later and told him that it not only absorbed the cat urine, it kept the smell down too. She wanted more. Her friends wanted some. Lowe realized he had something special.

Lowe called his new product "Kitty Litter" and packaged up five pound bags. When he first took it to store owners they declined to sell it because sand was so much cheaper. Lowe told them to give it away free, confident people would appreciate a good thing. They did and he ended up traveling all over the country selling Kitty Litter. He later developed the Tidy Cat brand that is still available in stores today.

Toilet Tissue

Some things are such a regular part of our lives that we take them for granted but virtually everything had to begin as an idea at some point. With that in mind great thanks is given for the creative mind of Joseph Gayetty. He was the inventor of what we now know as toilet paper. In 1857 he came up with the idea, packaged it and began to sell it in the United States. Gayetty took out an advertisement in Scientific American where he declared his toilet paper was a 'grand and unapproachable discovery' and 'the greatest blessing of our age'. When you stop and think about life without it, he may have been right.

"Gayetty's Medicated Paper" was sold in packages of flat sheets, medicated with aloe and watermarked with his name. In 1871 serious competition arrived, compliments of Seth Wheeler. Wheeler patented toilet paper rolls with perforated paper. That style became the industry standard and remains in use today, though the debate over whether the roll should be on the inside or the outside has never fully been settled.

Paper Towels

Two brothers, Arthur and Irvin Scott founded a company in 1879 and by 1907 the Scott Paper Company had become the number one American brand of toilet tissue. It was a happy accident that brought the creation of yet another product, paper towels. By mistake a batch of toilet tissue had been made with extremely thick rolls, essentially rendering it unsellable. About the same time a Philadelphia school teacher had started substituting soft paper for towels in the wash room. She did this in an effort to combat cold and flu season. Community towels would only further the spread of sickness whereas the soft paper could be thrown away after a single use.

Arthur Scott got wind of her idea and decided perhaps rather than throw out the useless toilet tissue, he could repurpose it. He had it cut into individual sections of towel sized sheets and marketed them as a preventative measure against disease. He named them Sani-Towels. The initial run went well and Scott determined there was a market for them. He successfully sold them to hotels and restaurants for use in their rest rooms. Demand never stopped growing. A late 19th century production mistake created what is now a $5.3 billion dollar a year U.S. paper towel market.

Scuba Diving

Swimming underwater for hours at a time seemed like an impossibly absurd idea for most of the history of mankind. Then came Henry William. William was awarded the first patent for a rebreather apparatus in 1878. It was part of scuba gear he designed that allowed a diver to stay underwater for as long as three hours.

In 1943 Frenchmen Jaques Cousteau and Emile Gagnan created and perfected a scuba diving system that would supply divers with compressed air when they breathed. The same basic system is used by scuba divers today. Cousteau would go on to produce countless movies and television programs introducing people to the world under the sea, including Oscar winning films. His work inspired future generations of scuba exploration and brought the sea to those who couldn't dive themselves.

Sunscreen

In modern American culture, spending time relaxing at the beach, on a boat or enjoying other outdoor recreational pursuits rank among America's favorite leisure activities. Not everyone's skin is suited for extended exposure to the sun however. Enter sunscreen.

Austrian Franz Greiter suffered a serious sunburn while mountain climbing at Piz Buin in the late 1930s. As a result he became determined to find a way to protect his skin for future outings. In 1946 he created his first version of what we now know as sunscreen. There is some disagreement as to whether he was actually the first to create an effective sun protection. In 1944 a Florida airman and pharmacist named Benjamin Green created a product to protect the skin of World War II soldiers serving in the Pacific tropics. His patented formula was red, sticky and about the same viscosity as petroleum jelly. It did protect the skin but wasn't a practical sell to the public so after the war Green began to blend cocoa butter and coconut oil in to make it more appealing. Coppertone bought Green's patent, tinkered with the formula and successfully marketed it in the 1950s as the "Bain de Soleil" and "Coppertone Girl" brands.

Greiter invented the SPF rating system for sunscreens in 1962. The greater the SPF number, the longer a person can safely stay in the sun. Today a broad spectrum sunscreen with an SPF of 30 or above will block 96% of the sun's harmful rays. Most sunscreens are water resistant, meaning they won't wash away even if you swim.

Teddy Bears
A Teddy Bear is a stuffed toy bear intended to bring comfort and joy, most commonly to children. The first bears were created in 1902 by Richard Steiff for the German based Steiff toy company. His aunt Margarete owned the company. She wasn't particularly keen on his bear idea, but placated her nephew by allowing him to produce one hundred bears and take them to the 1903 Leipzig Toy Fair. An American buyer bought all one hundred and ordered another three thousand. The next year the Steiff company attended the St. Louis World's Fair. They received the Gold Medal for their bears and sold twelve thousand of the stuffed critters on the spot. By 1907, almost one million teddy bears had been sold.

Since the early 1950s, bear sales have typically been on the order of one quarter of a million bears per year. The name "Teddy" bear originally came from President Theodore Roosevelt and has pretty much defined stuffed bears ever since.

If you are looking to get a Teddy Bear for your child or your sweetheart they are typically priced anywhere from $10 to $50. For collectors however, the price can be considerably higher. The ten most expensive Teddy Bears ever are all Steiff bears. All have sold at auction for ridiculous sums of money. In the year 2000 luxury brand Louis Vuitton partnered with Steiff to create the world's most expensive bear. Wearing a designer coat and hat and accompanied by a miniature Louis Vuitton suit case, the bear sold at a charity auction for an unfathomable $2.1 million.

The Milkshake

America's love affair with milkshakes is legendary. Ice cream, milk and flavored syrup, carefully blended together, bring many people back to simpler days of their childhood and sharing the sweet treat with their high school sweetheart. The image of a milkshake is often used in classic movies for the purpose of evoking a sense of goodness and innocence. The original milkshakes however, were anything but innocent.

In 1885 the term milkshake referred to an eggnog like drink made with whiskey, not at all suitable for high school dates sharing a straw. It wasn't until 1922 that the cold delicious liquid snack universally recognized as a milkshake came into being. Ivar "Pop" Coulson was a soda jerk at Walgreens. He was always creating new and different treats. One day he decided he could improve on the chocolate malts of the day. His original recipe was milk, chocolate syrup and a spoonful of malt powder. It was okay, but something seemed to be missing. One day Pop tried adding one additional ingredient and realized he had something special. The ingredient? Ice cream. Apparently Pop got it right. Nearly one hundred years later, Walgreens no longer features a soda fountain, but tens of millions of milkshakes are sold each year.

Mark your calendar because September 12 is National Chocolate Milkshake Day.

ABOUT THE AUTHOR

Tim Constantine is an accomplished talk radio host, a frequent television pundit and an award winning writer at The Washington Times. His uncanny ability to hone in on the seemingly obvious yet often neglected reasoning behind political positions has proven to be an essential element in his recipe for success.

Constantine first hit the radio airwaves at age 13. At the time his deep voice didn't match his skinny frame and sneakers but through the magic of radio, it really didn't matter. As a young man he worked in Rock and Top 40 formats. Later, while serving in elected office, Constantine returned to broadcasting, this time in the Talk Radio format. The return was a smashing success. His show increased the station listeners in his time slot seven-fold. Perhaps most impressively, within 6 months of going on-air in the Talk format, Tim was consistently beating the previous #1 talk show, hosted by a 15 year talk radio veteran.

Today Constantine broadcasts from Washington DC to listeners all across the United States. He combines his background in TV and radio, his experience in public office, his controversial fall from grace and his hard-nosed business approach with his understated sense of humor for one of the most entertaining radio programs anywhere. His award winning work for The Washington Times is read across the country and around the globe.

His conservative beliefs don't stop him from questioning the motives and effectiveness of politicians of all stripes. Never mean, but always seeking truth and accuracy, Constantine is a breath of fresh air in today's world of mindless talking points from the left or the right.

Learn more at www.TimConstantine.com

WHITE GUYS ARE OKAY TOO

CPSIA information can be obtained
at www.ICGtesting.com
Printed in the USA
LVHW041258010920
664636LV00004B/329